DAILY DOSE OF
ENCOURAGEMENT
FOR LIFE'S JOURNEY

Ugochi Agbasimelo

Printed and bound in the UK by CLOC Ltd

First Edition

ISBN: 978-1-8383564-2-2 (Paperback)

Appreciation

I want to say a big thank you to my LORD Jesus Christ who loved me and gave His life for me. He has also empowered me and enabled me to write this book. He has given me unusual strength through many difficult situations and filled my heart with joy, peace and the sweet assurance that He will never let me fall. Dear Jesus, I am very grateful. Thank You for Your faithfulness.

I want to thank my husband, Pastor Charles Agbasimelo, my children - Robert and Chiso Arthur and Kene Agbasimelo – they are truly wonderful gifts. I call them 'my precious ones'.

I am grateful to my mother – the matriarch of the Odocha/Njoku clan, for her support, zest for life and inspiration – nothing stops her from achieving her goals. Thank you, Mummy.

My siblings have been awesome, particularly my sisters – simply phenomenal. No words can describe their strength and the weight of support they gave me when I needed it most. Chioma and Chiso, thank you.

My thanks also to Okey (Chioma's husband), Chino and Chidi (my brothers) and Ifey (Chidi's wife).

I am so very grateful for the tremendous support I received from my pastor and spiritual father, Pastor Taiwo Odukoya, who, amid his pain and struggle, constantly reached out to see how I was doing. Thank you, Sir. You know I love and appreciate you.

I have friends and colleagues too numerous to mention who have been sterling and mind-blowing in their regard for me – it can only be God and I am grateful to them and to God for making it possible for our paths to cross this side of heaven.

I must acknowledge my wonderful sister and 'daughter in the Lord' who, when I mentioned this book, took it upon herself to start compiling some of the messages and sermons I have preached over the years. My darling Lady Desh (Mrs Desola Oluwasanya), thank you and to your amazing husband who supported you during the tedious weeks and months of putting a selection together, without complaining, thank you Doc Sola.

My prayer is that anyone who reads all or part of these encouraging words will find the strength to keep going. To take one more step, keep believing and know that there is nothing our God cannot do.

Life happens – but in Christ we are equipped for victory.

You are running a race you are destined to win.

Be blessed, folks.

Agape ❣ xx

PU

Dedication

This book is dedicated to Mr Bethel Chinweoke Njoku, who during great suffering, remained cheerful and loving to the very end.

A man who gave more than he had, generous to a fault and taught us the value of people over and above possessions.

Known by many as Chy, Daddy, Granddad, Dee Bethel, Big Daddy, Brother, Uncle, Onye-Nkuzi, Kojak, Bethel. He was wise, dignified and confident through challenges, yet modest in success.

Thank you, daddy, for your great legacy.

Bethel Chinweoke Njoku aka BCN (1934 – 2017).

Table of contents

DAY-TO-DAY MOTIVATION

Introduction

Life happens, period.

That we are Christians, does not give us immunity from life's vicissitudes. However, being Christian does help us see all that happening from a Godward perspective and enables us to walk life's journey with strength, joy, peace and assurance that God will not let us fall.

This book was written to bring encouragement to people everywhere who are going through one challenge or the other and are a little perplexed as to why. Especially people of faith – the Christian faith.

The concepts in the book are what I firmly believe in and the core of what drives my actions and behaviours.

I pray it blesses you and you find encouragement during those tough times. There is one encouraging narrative for each day and you can dip in and out as necessary.

Be blessed.

God-Given Ability

Now the gates of Jericho were securely barred because of the Israelites. No one went out and no one came in. Then the Lord said to Joshua, "See, I have delivered Jericho into your hands, along with its king and its fighting men. March around the city once with all the armed men. Do this for six days. Have seven priests carry trumpets of rams' horns in front of the ark. On the seventh day, march around the city seven times, with the priests blowing the trumpets. When you hear them sound a long blast on the trumpets, have the whole army give a loud shout; then the wall of the city will collapse and the army will go up, everyone straight in." ... When the trumpets sounded, the army shouted, and at the sound of the trumpet, when the men gave a loud shout, the wall collapsed; so, everyone charged straight in, and they took the city (Joshua 6:1-4, 20; NIV).

When an event or feat is described as supernatural, it means whatever was achieved or happened cannot be explained by the laws of nature. The Bible is replete with supernatural events orchestrated and executed by God. God, in His infinite wisdom, endowed some individuals and groups of people with the ability to achieve supernatural feats.

The event in Joshua chapter 6 is one such occurrence. This event and others like it tell us that supernatural ability comes from God. It is God-dependent. If God promises to do anything, He is solely responsible for bringing it to pass. All we have to do is follow His instructions, do what He would have us do, and be where He would have us be. God provides the power, plans the process, and performs the supernatural in line with His purpose and will. When God endows us with a supernatural ability for a task or purpose, we must not make the mistake of thinking that we have done something to earn this awesome privilege. If we think so, that is, think this supernatural ability is down to us, we will not go far.

When we depend on God for supernatural ability to bring about major necessary shifts in our lives, our good, kind, and powerful God will put into process whatever He needs to do to ensure that we win. In this same Book of Joshua, there was war between the Israelites and the Amorites. God fought for Israel that day by using hailstones and extending daylight for as long as daylight was needed for the battle. The Bible says, *"The sun stopped in the middle of the sky and delayed going down about a full day"* (Joshua 10:13[b]).

God is the possessor of all skills, and there is nothing He cannot do. Joshua had a huge task of taking multitudes of people numbering more than two million to the Promised Land. Our "Promised Land" today is each day God gives us. Every new day is a challenge/battleground, but I want you to know that as God was with Joshua, He is also with you. Also, note that the Israelites only had to walk around the wall and shout when asked to on the seventh day, and the wall fell. They obeyed the instructions God gave them.

God always gave Joshua assuring words of victory each time he faced opposition. And as God spoke to Joshua, God is speaking to us today. He is telling us that the battle has already been won. All we need to do is receive our victory. Please, note that the process may not always be the same, so we must listen and be attentive to God's words and the instructions He is giving us.

God gave Joshua different instructions for various challenges.

For Jericho, Joshua was told to match around the city for seven days; please, note that the seventh-day instruction was different from the other six days!

For the coalition army that attacked the Israelites' neighbours, the Gibeonites, Joshua was asked to go out to war and face them, but though they went into battle, God fought for them with hailstones and extended the day for as long as was needed. That is why we need to be attentive to what God is always saying to us so we can position ourselves and obtain victory.

As Joshua made himself available, we must also make ourselves available. As we do this, we will, like Joshua, conquer Jericho. What is our "Jericho" today? It can be our fear, anger, guilt, anxiety, bitterness, prejudice, and so on. It is an attitude or mindset that keeps us from our joy and peace. I want to remind us that the same power which raised Jesus from the dead is still available to those who believe.

All we need do is listen to God and take up the positions He has asked us to. This may not always be easy to do, but God is saying to us today, just as He said to Joshua, *"Be strong and courageous"*. You see, we may need the courage to take up the positions God has called us to lay hold of because these positions may mean doing away with some attitudes, friends, or prized possessions. It may require reaching out to someone who had hurt you, forgiving someone, and loving the unlovable.

The good news is that God supplies supernatural ability; He provides the power, plans the process, and performs the victory. All we have to do is yield.

We are Able Because God is More than Able!

The Lord turned to him and said, "Go in the strength you have and save Israel out of Midian's hand. Am I not sending you?" "Pardon me, my lord," Gideon replied, "but how can I save Israel? My clan is the weakest in Manasseh, and I am the least in my family." **(Judges 6:14-15; NIV)**

I now understand that God cannot love us more than He already does. Anything God does through us is driven by His love for us. So, when we go through unbearable situations (you may be going through one now), I'd like to remind us that even in such cases, God is with us ALL THE WAY. God is with us in them. He is right in there with us and will not leave us there. If we are not where we'd like to be right now, it is not because we are faithless, abandoned, or unloved. God paid a huge price for us and has called us to Him. Anyone who has answered that call belongs to Him, and no one and nothing can snatch us from Him.

The Bible leads me to understand that it is never about our ability but God's. Therefore, we only need to make ourselves available to Him.

When God told Gideon to go in the strength he (Gideon) had, Gideon was convinced his strength and status would not be able to deliver what God requested of him, but the truth is our God can bring about mighty feats with little or much. For example, our Lord Jesus fed over 5000 people with a little boy's lunch of five loaves and two fish. When Jesus asked Philip where they would get enough food to feed the multitude, the Bible records that Jesus *'knew what He was going to do'*. In the same way, God knew what He had planned to do for the Israelites through Gideon, despite his strength and pedigree.

When God calls us, He already knows how to execute what He wants to do through us. He can do more than we can possibly ask or think according to His power at work in us.

The thousands who were fed had their fill according to their want, and there were twelve baskets leftover! It started with a little boy making what he had available. Likewise, Gideon learned to make what he had available. We need to learn to bring what we have—our talent, time, and substance—no matter how small we think they are and give them to God for His use. He has the ability to multiply it so that all can get blessed by the gifts we have handed over to God. We all have something to start with. Don't keep it to yourself! We may have doubts as Gideon did, but he obeyed, and so must we.

All that's required of us is our obedience and yielding. Our ability to fulfil purpose has nothing to do with us (the vessel) but God, who will use us to bless those He wants us to reach.

For those of us who still have lingering doubts, feeling we don't have what it takes to do what we believe God is nudging us to do, I ask you to trust God and give Him what you have.

He can use it to achieve more than you ever imagined, with loads left over. He will bless you in the process too.

Let us borrow a leaf from the story of Joseph (Genesis 40). After Joseph had interpreted the dreams of Pharaoh's cupbearer and baker who were in prison with him, he asked the cupbearer to put in a good word for him with Pharaoh, saying, "...I was forcibly carried off...I have done nothing to deserve being put in a dungeon." This shows we can honestly acknowledge where we are and what we need. However, we must resist the temptation to let the situation weigh us down. Though Joseph felt the pain of the injustice, he still ministered to those around him. He also understood that his place was not to know 'how' or 'when' but to just keep on trusting God. God will bring major, mega deliverances through us; we just need to be wise enough to give Him what we have, no matter how little we think it is. God is able to expand our capacity beyond our wildest dreams because of His supernatural power that works in us.

DAY THREE

Chosen to Shine

Arise, Shine, for your light has come!

I came across this story about a bird that somehow finds its way into a church building:

"Every once in a while, we get a bird inside this sanctuary. It doesn't really want to be in here, but it's trapped. We don't want the bird in here because it can be messy and disruptive in worship. Do you know how the facilities department gets a bird out of this huge room? They don't put out poison birdseed or take a shotgun to it. The goal is not to destroy but to release. The solution is simple. They turn out all the lights until it's pitch-black and then turn on a bright light on an exit hallway, and the bird instinctively flies to the light" (Bob Russell Southeast Christian Church in Louisville, KY).

Jesus said, *"I am the light of the world. Whoever follows me will never walk in darkness but will have the light of life"* (John 8:12). We were once darkness, but then we have seen The Great Light (our Lord Jesus Christ).

Apostle Paul writing to the Ephesians, said, *"For you were once darkness, but now you are light in the Lord. Live as children of light."*

We must let our light shine so that our **good** deeds will be seen, and Jehovah God will be praised. Giving the credit or praise back to God, in the Christian context, after good deeds, means we have made it clear from the outset that Our Lord Jesus Christ is our source. It shows we cannot take any credit for the good deed done. That's how it should be—it's all about Jesus; He is the Light that has come. He is the Light we shine through.

To shine, we must connect to the main light source. We do this by staying close in worship, Bible study, prayer, and acts of faith. However, we must not dim or extinguish our light with a blanket of sin.

It is essential we keep our gaze and focus on the Light source, looking unto Jesus, the author and pioneer of our faith. We must believe He is and keep believing, no matter the odds. A strong blindfold is unbelief; it blinds us, and we can no longer see the Light. God forbid that we walk in unbelief in any area of our lives. Apostle Paul said to the Corinthian church – *"The god of this age has blinded the minds of unbelievers, so that they cannot see the light of the gospel of the glory of Christ, who is the image of God"* (2 Corinthians 4:4).

Our prayer is, "May our light shine so brightly that it penetrates their blindness and releases them from the darkness and destruction of sin. In the Mighty Name of Jesus Christ".

Jesus Christ says to us in Matthew 5:14-16 (Message Bible):

"You're here to be light, bringing out the God-colours in the world. God is not a secret to be kept. We're going public with this, as public as a city on a hill. If I make you light-bearers, you don't think I'm going to hide you under a bucket, do you? I'm putting you on a light stand. Now that I've put you there on a hilltop, on a light stand—shine! Keep open house; be generous with your lives. By opening up to others, you'll prompt people to open up with God, this generous Father in heaven."

So, my dear brother and sister-in-Christ, understand clearly that you have been chosen to shine—so SHINE!

Light up the Path

¹In the beginning God created the heavens and the earth. ²Now the earth was formless and empty, darkness was over the surface of the deep, and the Spirit of God was hovering over the waters.

³ And God said, "Let there be light," and there was light. ⁴ God saw that the light was good, and he separated the light from the darkness. ⁵ God called the light "day," and the darkness he called "night." And there was evening, and there was morning—the first day. (Genesis 1:1-5; NIV)

I would like to highlight a couple of things from this passage. Firstly, when there was no order (chaos and emptiness), God called forth light, and it was good. Jesus called us the light of the world; this means we are 'good'. This implies that we are capable of bringing good to any bad situation. That's truly awesome. This is what we have been created for— to bring good to situations without order, circumstances that are chaotic and seem empty (void). We are the solution; therefore, we must shine as we should. We need to live up to our character.

Secondly, God called for a separation between light and darkness—once light was created and God saw that the light was good, the first thing he did was to separate them. This tells me the two cannot co-exist; there's either darkness or light. Light and darkness cannot mix. Light, no matter how dim, will always trump darkness. He called light 'day' and darkness 'night'. We belong to the day; listen to the following...

You are all sons of the light and sons of the day. We do not belong to the night or to the darkness. So then, let us not be like others, who are asleep, but let us be alert and self-controlled. For those who sleep, sleep at night, and those who get drunk, get drunk at night. But since we belong to the day, let us be self-controlled, putting on faith and love as a breastplate, and the hope of salvation as a helmet. For God did not appoint us to suffer wrath but to receive salvation through our Lord Jesus Christ. He died for us so that, whether we are awake or asleep, we may live together with him. Therefore encourage one another and build each other up, just as in fact you are doing (1 Thessalonians 5:5-11; NIV).

The onus is on us to actively arise and shine, be self-controlled, putting on faith and love as a breastplate. 'Arise' is an action word; 'putting on' is an action word, so we cannot remain passive or static. As God's grace propels us, we must make every effort to keep close to the 'Light Source'. We must throw off everything that hinders us and run the race marked out for us.

Our light is the unadulterated bright light from the Son Himself. Hear this: *"There will be **no more night.** They will not need the light of a lamp or the light of the sun, for the Lord God will give them light. And they will reign forever and ever!"* (Revelations 22:5).

We do not need a lampshade, nor do we need a coloured bulb. We shine with the Son's Light; we are separate from darkness, and when we step into a situation, light illuminates the path and brings about desired solutions. We are a unique breed of light bearers; we are of God and shine we must.

DAY FIVE

God wants to, and He will

Please, read a few portions of scripture with me and note the emphasis on some phrases,

*"**Don't bargain with God. Be direct. Ask for what you need.** This isn't a cat-and-mouse, hide-and-seek game we're in. If your child asks for bread, do you trick him with sawdust? If he asks for fish, do you scare him with a live snake on his plate? As bad as you are, you wouldn't think of such a thing. You're at least decent to your own children. So don't you think the God who conceived you in love will be even better?"* (Matthew 7:7-11; MSG)

*"**As the Father has loved me, so have I loved you.** Now remain in my love"* (John 15:9; NIV).

*What, then, shall we say in response to this? If God is for us, who can be against us? He who did not spare his own Son, but gave him up for us all — **how will he not also, along with him, graciously give us all things?*** (Romans 8:31-32; NIV).

*Jesus looked at them intently and said, "Humanly speaking, it is impossible. But not with God. **Everything is possible with God**"* (Mark 10:27-28; NLT).

The Bible passages we have read above and the emphasis (mine) demonstrate that God is willing and able to meet our needs. So, when we come before Him in prayer, there is no need to be anxious. Getting our needs met is His responsibility; He is a responsible Father, and He will do it. The phrases I emphasised constantly remind me that our part is to respond to His love.

All it entails is to ask for what we need. There's no need to start bargaining with the Holy of Holies if He did not spare His only Son in bringing about our redemption. Then we need to ask ourselves, how won't He, along with our Lord Jesus Christ, give us all we ask for?

So, let us approach our God as He would have us do. We see the pattern laid out when   our Lord Jesus taught His disciples to pray:

² And He said to them, "When you pray, say: *Our* Father *Who is in heaven*, hallowed be Your name, Your kingdom come. *Your will be done [held holy and revered] on earth as it is in heaven.*

³ Give us daily our bread [food for the morrow].

⁴ And forgive us our sins, for we ourselves also forgive everyone who is indebted to us [who has offended us or done us wrong]. And bring us not into temptation *but rescue us from evil* (Luke 11:2-4; AMPC).

Our Father - There must be a relationship, a close loving relationship; you do not call someone you do not know 'my father'!

Hallowed be Your name - We need to acknowledge His Person that He is God and there is no other. Therefore, he is to be worshipped and revered.

Your kingdom come; Your will be done - His desires must trump our needs. So, it is not the Father succumbing to our wants, needs, and desires, but us bringing our will in line with His. Jesus put this another way when He said, *'Seek first his kingdom and his righteousness, and all these things will be given to you as well'* (Matthew 6:33). The Psalmist was also astute to this truth because he encourages us to *'delight ourselves in the Lord and He will grant us the desires of our heart'*! (Psalm 37:4).

Give us daily our bread – Then we ask that our needs be met—whatever they may be—spiritual, physical, financial, emotional, and mental wellbeing—whatever!

And forgive us our sins, for we ourselves also forgive everyone…Back to relationships, we cannot run away from this. We must strive to see that our relationships are on a good footing as long as this depends on us. Jehovah expects that our relationships are free of resentment, bitterness, and negative feelings.

And bring us not into temptation…Once our relationships are well established, we can now ask for protection.

One last word from the Master's mouth: *"Let us then approach the throne of grace with confidence that we may receive mercy and find grace to help us in our time of need"*.

Our God is **VERY** willing to meet our needs; you only need to ask.

Heritage of the Righteous

So, who is righteous? What does it mean to be righteous? Let us see how the dictionary (online dictionary) defines the word 'righteous':

> Morally upright; without guilt or sin
>
> In accordance with virtue or morality
>
> Morally justifiable

These are clearly adjectives and, by the look of them, a tall order. Is there anyone of us who can look back on our day and honestly say we have been entirely morally upright, without guilt or sin? Can we say all our actions have been virtuous and of great morality? That all our thoughts, deeds, and words spoken so far have been morally justifiable?

If anyone reads this and says, "yes", then I will confidently conclude that you woke up less than a minute ago, or you are either extremely economical with the truth or lack insight. Jokes apart, no one can lay hold of being 100% completely righteous at any given day or time. However, the Bible does have some insight into how we can confidently and boldly claim to be in the camp of those called 'righteous'. There are quite a few Bible passages that give us this insight, but I will focus on the following from the Book of 2nd Corinthians.

God made him who had no sin to be sin for us, so that in him we might become the righteousness of God (2 Corinthians 5:21; NIV).

As those called and chosen by our Lord Jesus Christ, we have this awesome, mind-blowing truth, 'we are God's righteousness'. The Holy God who abhors sin got His Son to be sin for us so that we will become His righteousness! What an amazing truth, what an amazing gift, and what an amazing God!

And do you know something else? As the righteousness of God, we have a beautiful heritage. In Psalm 34, the Psalmist gives us a clue into what our heritage resembles.

The eyes of the Lord are on the righteous and his ears are attentive to their cry (Psalm 34:15).

God has His focus on you, so pay attention to your every word. Please, speak to Him if you are truly burdened and need to cry or let off steam. Feel free to do so to Jehovah God. Shed those tears into the palm of His hand.

The righteous cry out, and the Lord hears them; he delivers them from all their problems (Psalms 34:17).

The righteous are not immune from troubles and problems. The troubles will come; it is not a matter of 'if' but 'when'. The good news is that it doesn't end with the onslaught of the troubles/problems but that our good and merciful God delivers us from them all. ALL, not just a few, or most, but ALL. Don't suffer in silence; follow the Psalmist's example and cry out. Cry out to the LORD and Him alone. *This is our confidence, that He hears us. And if we know that He hears us—whatever we ask—we know that we have what we asked of Him,* so Apostle John tells us in 1 John 5:14-15.

A righteous man may have many troubles, but the Lord delivers him from them all, he protects all his bones, not one of them will be broken (Psalms 34:19-20).

This verse really excites me; I understand from this verse that when God delivers us from problems, we are delivered whole. The core of who we are remains intact. We do not limp into victory; our bones are not broken. We can rejoice, dance, leap, jump, and hop without broken bones into our place of deliverance.

Evil will slay the wicked; the foes of the righteous will be condemned (Psalms 34:21).

God will ensure that evil (darkness) will not have the upper hand. He will war against our foes (our enemies) and defeat their hold over us. God has spoken; He calls us His righteousness in Christ Jesus and has given us an awesome heritage as a result.

Praise the Most High God!

Called to Serve

"The God who made the world and everything in it, this Master of sky and land...doesn't...need the human race to run errands for him, as if he couldn't take care of himself. He makes the creatures; the creatures don't make him..." (Acts 17:24-25; MSG)

Sometimes, we offer our service to God as if He needs us to do things for Him that He could not do Himself, forgetting He spoke the world into existence. Whatever we do, we cannot add or subtract from His greatness, power, glory, and supremacy. The stark truth is that God doesn't need our work, money, worship, or praise—has this shocked you?

Let us think about it—God, who made the heavens and earth, surely can get anything He needs done without us. He owns every animal of the forest and the cattle on a thousand hills; the world is His and everything in it (Psalms 50:10-12). Therefore, he does not need our praises to bolster His ego or self-esteem.

So, the question is this, "Why are we commanded in scripture to serve, praise, worship, and give cheerfully and generously?" The answer? It's for our own benefit. Yes, we get back from God when we serve, praise, worship, and give. We add nothing to Him, but He adds plenty to us.

We manifest His glory by our obedience to serve, worship, praise, and give. This creates an atmosphere of blessings, of which we are partakers. The Bible tells us in the Book of 2 Chronicles, chapter 7, how Solomon dedicated the temple he built with extravagant worship and got a visitation from God. This visitation affirmed God's covenant of mercy, favour, protection, and goodwill for Solomon and the Israelites.

In the Book of 1ˢᵗ Peter, Apostle Peter tells us that we are a chosen people, a royal priesthood, a holy nation, God's special possession, called forth to show (manifest, declare) God's praises, in other words, declare His Glory (1 Peter 2:9-10).

We show our love for God by obeying His commands; our obedience causes us to manifest His glory, and His covenant of mercy kicks in. We get all we need for life and godliness.

The Bible shows us how God used a myriad of different people and personalities; it did not depend on their ability or comeliness to bring about His divine purpose. For instance, He chose David to defeat Goliath and Mary to give birth to Jesus Christ. When God chooses, He empowers; so, the enablement is not of the chosen but of Him who chose. When our Lord Jesus Christ came, He demonstrated this character of God by choosing a bunch of 12 men to walk closely with Him. These men had diverse temperaments, abilities, and learnedness, but Jesus used them all (including Judas) to bring about the desired end.

So, let us stop asking, "Can I?" "Me?" "Would God really use me?" All we need to do is commit to loving Him by our obedience to serve, worship, praise, and give. Then, we will see His hand at work in us and our circumstances.

Let us take heart from the account of those whom Jesus chose to be His closest companions—those who would carry on His work. They changed the world not because of what they had in themselves but because of the One who empowered them. And they were part of something extraordinary.

Today, we are also part of something wonderful. We must no longer sit still on the pews. Instead, we must get up and serve, worship, praise, and give. As we do these and whatever else our generous God prompts us to do, the heavens will surely open over us perpetually.

Press through to your Victory

Do not be anxious about anything, but in every situation, by prayer and petition, with thanksgiving, present your requests to God. And the peace of God, which transcends all understanding, will guard your hearts and your minds in Christ Jesus (Philippians 4:6-7; NIV).

A cursory study of the Bible will establish the fact that true progress (advancement) is made when we persist and push through obstacles, i.e., fight some life battles. A well-known example is told in 2 Chronicles, chapter 20, about Jehoshaphat, a king of Judah. Jehoshaphat received news that a vast army, an alliance of three nations, was on its way to Judah to attack them. Despite his fear and dread, the story ends well; the vast army is defeated, and Jehoshaphat ends up with huge plunder.

Let's see how Jehoshaphat went from fear and dread to becoming a conqueror.

The account of this event starts by telling us that Jehoshaphat was shaken, alarmed, fearful, and terrified, but he resolved to ask God for help. In that state of fear, he called a fast, prayed, and told the whole nation to join him. I like the fact that he asked the whole nation to join him. Of course, we should always seek to be alone with God in prayer, but this also tells us that there is a time when we have to come together as a community to pray—corporate prayer as we like to call it. Jehoshaphat led this prayer meeting. Let's look at the pattern of his prayer and see what we can glean from it.

- He committed the situation to God, acknowledging God's power to save.

- He sought God's favour because he knew the people of Judah were God's people.

- He acknowledged God's sovereignty over the current situation.

- He praised God's glory and took comfort in His promises.

- He professed complete dependence on God, not Himself, for deliverance.

The point is that these prayers brought them to a place of prophecy and an assurance of God's supernatural intervention. Jehoshaphat's prayer introduced Jehovah into the situation.

Whenever we encounter what seems like an insurmountable challenge, we may want to follow Jehoshaphat's example and believe it is now time for God to act and man to rest. We will have peace amid our numerous challenges if we realise that the battle is not ours but God's. We must recognise our human limitations and allow God's strength to work through our fears and weaknesses. It is also good to ensure we are pursuing God's interests and not just our own selfish desires.

Let us ask God for help in our daily battles. The challenges we face will wear different faces and come in different shapes and degrees of difficulty. We'll battle all sorts of temptations and pressures daily, but we can have peace and joy by resting our confidence on our God. He will work on our weaknesses and bring us to a place of victory in Jesus Christ's Mighty Name.

Jehoshaphat, an Old Testament saint, understood this. We of the New Covenant in Christ Jesus should have greater understanding and peace because of what the blood of Jesus Christ has bought for us.

In this new dispensation, our Father in heaven, who is very rich in mercy and grace (I call these the currency of heaven), lavishes this currency on us here on earth. The Bible tells us that His mercy triumphs over justice. So, whatever the situation is, we must not allow the enemy to use our past mistakes to hold us back and bind us to fear and dread.

A lot of us refuse to go forward because of our past mistakes. There is nobody without past mistakes. We need to press ahead regardless of the mistakes. God has lavished grace on us. Whatever we need, we only need to call on God, and there is a sure prophecy for us. That prophecy is that worry is banished from us.

God will fight the battle, but He wants you to take your position (in Him, by prayer and faith) and stand firm.

A Peep into God's Awesome Power

There is a portion of scripture that allows us to peep into God's awesome power.

We read of His awesome power when He delivered the Israelites from the Egyptian army by parting the Red Sea, allowing the Israelites to walk on dry ground and drowning Pharaoh's army in the same place the Israelites had crossed. Indeed, God's power is awesome. We see Jesus demonstrate this power in the miraculous healings He performed. One of such miracles is the raising of Lazarus from the dead and calming raging storms. Yes! God's power is awesome.

One of my many go-to scriptures is Ephesians 3:14-21 (NIV):

*[14] For this reason I kneel before the Father, [15] from Whom every family in heaven and on earth derives its name. [16] I pray that out of His glorious riches He may strengthen you with **power** through His Spirit in your inner being, [17] so that Christ may dwell in your hearts through faith. And I pray that you, being rooted and established in love, [18] may have **power**, together with all the Lord's holy people, to grasp how wide and long and high and deep is the love of Christ, [19] and to know this love that surpasses knowledge—that you may be filled to the measure of all the fullness of God.*

*20 Now to Him Who is able to do immeasurably more than all we ask or imagine, according to His **power** that is at work within us, 21 to Him be glory in the church and in Christ Jesus throughout all generations, for ever and ever! Amen.*

In the New International Version (NIV) quoted above, the word **power** comes up thrice in these eight verses.

Verse 16: - I pray that out of His glorious riches, He may strengthen you with **power**…

Verse 18: - may have **power**…

Verse 20: - …according to His **power** that is at work…

The Greek scholars tell us that the Greek word, 'dunamis', is translated as power in verses 16 and 20, whereas the Greek word 'exischuo' (pronounced exiskhoo) is translated as power in verse 18. Dunamis (as in dynamite) speaks of 'force' which produces a force that shifts and brings forth; for example, miracles. *Exischuo* speaks of having 'full strength' (full strength to understand and grasp a love beyond human understanding).

Just as Apostle Paul prayed for the Ephesian church with these words, we should also pray these words into our lives. When we pray them, we are releasing power at full strength for the miraculous in our lives—power (dunamis) to shift the seemingly impossible situations we face. It will bring about the glorious turnaround we so desperately need, bring to life the dream we had killed and buried, and see God's grace and mercy manifest unusually in our lives. It is vital we are constantly praying these words so that we can take up all God will have us get.

There are five truths about the power we need to keep in mind daily:

Purpose – Power has a definite purpose. To bring about salvation, deliverance, restoration, redemption, and so on

Obedience – God's power in our life is activated by obedience. The incident of a poor widow in 1 Kings 17 is reported. As she is known, this widow of Zarephath was commanded by God to feed Prophet Elijah. When Elijah reached her and asked for a meal, she offered her last meal— she planned to have this last meal with her son and wait for death! But at Elijah's instruction, she prepared this 'last' meal for Elijah, and we are told her jar of flour and jug of oil did not run dry until the famine ended. Not only that, her son died but was raised to life by God's power. When we are obedient, even when we find ourselves between a rock and a hard place, it will not be a dead end because God's power will come through for us.

The **Word** – There is power in God's Word. The Bible tells us that *"the Son is the radiance of God's glory…sustaining all things by His powerful Word"* (Hebrews 1:3). We are also informed that the Word of God is alive and active. It is sharper than any double-edged sword, penetrating even to the dividing of soul and spirit, joints and marrow. It judges the thoughts and attitudes of the heart (Hebrews 4:12). Jesus told us (in Matthew 7:24) that by listening and keeping His word, we will be able to withstand the vagaries of life with peace and poise.

Encouragement – The display of God's power in our lives brings great encouragement. When Paul, his companions, and jailors were shipwrecked on the island of Malta, God displayed His tremendous power through Paul by delivering him from the bite of a poisonous snake. Through him, God brought healing to many on the Island (Acts 28:1-10). This led the Islanders to treat Paul and his companions exceptionally well with great hospitality.

Results – God's power in our lives brings great, tremendous results. Examples abound in the Bible—Joshua defeating an army of five nations (Joshua 10:1-11). God took over, brought about confusion in the enemies' army, and hurled large hailstones—*"…more of them died from the hail than were killed by the swords of the Israelites"* (Joshua 10:11). In addition, God's power brought about the healing of a man who was lame from birth, whose healing brought wonder and amazement to those who witnessed it. This event helped spread the Gospel of Jesus Christ to the world and continues to do so today.

So, let us hold these POWER truths close to our minds and hearts daily and take full possession of all that God's power entitles us as His children to have.

A Touch from God

I will state the obvious: "A touch from God changes lives." When Jehovah God touches us, we are completely transformed. Let us walk through Saul of Tarsus' encounter with God on his way to Damascus. God so changed his life that even his name was transformed from Saul to Paul.

Paul shares his testimony of encountering God with a crowd that had beaten him up and wanted to kill him. However, he had been saved from certain death by the intervention of the Roman soldiers at the time, and in Act 22:6, he says, *"About* **noon** *as I came near* **Damascus**, *suddenly a bright* **light** *from heaven flashed around me"*.

I have emphasised certain words with a significant meaning that will help us understand the importance of a touch from God and enable us to seek this experience with sincerity.

Paul tells about a bright light flashing around him (and at noon – when we expect very bright sun). This must have been some light! The Apostle John, speaking about our Lord Jesus, says, *"In Him was life, and that life was the Light of all mankind. The Light shines in the darkness, and the darkness has not overcome it…The true Light that gives light to everyone was coming into the world"* (John 1:4-5, 9).

This statement by Apostle John clearly shows us that our Lord Jesus Christ's life is our light. Jesus called us the light of the world and that we cannot be hidden. Therefore, we need to be shining and walking in the glow of His life and light—doing good deeds that His power and light enable us to do. When we shine, darkness will give way. Only good recognises the light; darkness doesn't. Paul recognised the Light (he asked, *'Who are you, Lord?'*). Paul was in some sort of darkness, persecuting followers of Christ, but when this bright light at noon-time shone around him, the darkness was dispelled, and Saul (now known as Paul) went on a different trajectory. So will our lives if we respond to the touch of God the same way Apostle Paul did.

We can pray for our loved ones (and the whole world) to receive a 'Damascus' experience, where the Light of God shines into their situation, enabling them to see the Lord and seek Him even more. He will answer that prayer and reveal Himself more.

The words *'noon'* and *'Damascus'* also have significance. This tells us that there is a time and place to receive divine touch. If truth be told, time is 'always'; time is 'now'. It's anytime we need a touch. The Psalmist says in Psalm 102:14 that our great God will arise and have compassion on Zion (you and me) and that the time to show us favour is now. Whenever we need God's touch is the right time. Great, isn't it?

It goes without saying that your 'Damascus'; my 'Damascus' is that place where and when we realise we really do need a touch from God. It is in the doctor's surgery when one has been given the news that they have cancer. It's at work when one has been told their job is at risk. It's any place when we really do need God to touch us and transform our situation. So, as you go about your business today—as Saul was, expect God's touch. He will give you a definitive experience that will lead to a much anticipated and definitive outcome.

In conclusion, just as Saul was transformed into powerful Paul when the Light of God touched him and his life was changed forever, for good, the same will be said of us whenever we seek and receive a divine touch from the Lord. His awesome power will transform and bring us into the reality of His glory in all areas of our lives. This will come to pass by His blood and in the Mighty Name of our Lord Jesus Christ. Amen.

Chillax! You are Jehovah's Child

¹² *But to as many as did receive and welcome Him, He gave the authority (power, privilege, right) to become the children of God, that is, to those who believe in (adhere to, trust in, and rely on) His name —*

¹³ *Who owe their birth neither to bloods nor to the will of the flesh [that of physical impulse] nor to the will of man [that of a natural father], but to God. [They are born of God!]* (John 1:12-13; Amplified, Classic Edition).

I love this portion of scripture very much. It gives me such a sense of assurance and confidence. I am God's child. It was His decision to make me His child, and He has conferred on me the authority, power, privilege, and right to call myself a child of God.

The beauty of this is that this is true and exciting for all of us who believe in the Lord Jesus Christ and have embraced Him as our Lord and Saviour.

As long as we remain God's own, He has given us the authority, power, and right to challenge the vicissitudes of life and come up trumps. This means we must train our minds and hearts to relax every time, even when things are not going so well. How do we get this training? Instead of worrying, we should let petitions and praises shape our worries into prayers. We must let God know our concerns, and God's peace that transcends all understanding will guard our hearts. We will then walk in this peace and into victory and wholeness.

We read in Isaiah 43 v 1:

But now, this is what the LORD says, He who created you Jacob, He who formed you, Israel: "Do not fear, for I have redeemed you; I have summoned you by name; you are Mine..."

Jacob and Israel are the same person. God changed Jacob's name (Jacob means supplanter, deceiver) to Israel (meaning – let God prevail; triumphant with God). This name change came about after Jacob had an encounter with God. In this encounter, Jacob wrestled with God. He insisted that he would not let God go until God blessed him. Through this encounter, Jacob showed that he was willing to let God triumph in his life and take the pre-eminence. Therefore, when Israel is called by his old name Jacob, Jehovah God affirms that He has chosen, redeemed, and protected him; hence, we should be encouraged. Whether we are being truly spiritual (as in Israel) or in a fleshly state (as in Jacob), God knows our name and has chosen us.

This may sound a bit controversial for some people, but the Bible tells us, *"For God so loved the world — (not "so loved the born-again Christians"), that He gave His only begotten Son."* God loves us regardless of our past. Sometimes, we the children of God, allow our weaknesses to hold us back. We must realise that whether we are seven days in Christ or 70 years, we will not reach the apex of Christian manifestation and character, this side of heaven. We are all 'work-in-progress'.

Understanding this—that we are all 'work-in-progress' gives us the encouragement and confidence we need to rebuff the attempts of Satan to keep us bound by guilt and immobilised by our past failures. The truth is that since God has got hold of us, He will never leave us where He found us. He will always lift us out of the mud and mire and set our feet on solid rock. Psalm 145:14 says, *"The LORD upholds all who fall and lifts up all who are bowed down."* Our LORD Jesus Christ is always 'washing our feet'. When Jesus Christ stooped to wash His disciples' feet, He made it clear that they were clean and only needed to have their feet washed after slugging it through the town. And so do we. We live in a fallen world, and our feet can get dirty at times—we need to get our feet washed by confessing and allowing the forgiveness that our Lord Jesus Christ offers make us whole again. As children of God who have been given the privilege, right, and authority to act and behave as God's children. We must not settle for anything less. We must not allow Satan to keep us standing in mud and mire. So, let's get our feet washed and move on.

God looked at us and decided to choose us. God be praised!

Child of God, Relax

It is a myth to think that our actions—good or bad—are without consequence.

The good news is that for us children of the Most High God, bought and washed by the blood of our Lord Jesus Christ, the rewards or consequences are for our ultimate good. It is exciting to note that as God's children, even when we misstep, God looks out for us.

Jesus made the following statements in John 6 verses 37 and 39 (Amplified Classic Edition):

37 All whom My Father gives (entrusts) to Me will come to Me; and the one who comes to Me I will most certainly not cast out [I will never, no never, reject one of them who comes to Me].

39 And this is the will of Him Who sent Me, that I should not lose any of all that He has given Me, but that I should give new life and raise [them all] up at the last day.

So, as we can see, our Lord Jesus Christ will clean us up and bring us back into the fold, but we must be willing and obedient. That is the only condition. The Bible is replete with accounts of how our Good and Mighty Jehovah looked out for

His chosen ones, even when they had clearly gone against His will and were being punished for their disobedience and waywardness.

Jeremiah 25 verse 12 tells how God declares that the Babylonian nation He sent to punish His children Israel will themselves be severely dealt with because they did not deal with His children with any iota of mercy.

Another account found in Ezra, chapter one, describes how our good and loving Father raised a King, Cyrus, who did not worship Him, to provide for the building of the temple. King Cyrus provided safe passage and material resources to ensure the temple of God was rebuilt.

We, who are blood-bought and washed, can really be at ease and peace because when God has called us His own, and we have heeded that call, He holds on to us forever. So, we can walk around with the confidence that God defends our corner and anyone who treats us with contempt, our Good God will sort them out.

The scripture says: *"Touch not my anointed"* and *"do my prophet no harm"*. If we are children of God, we are anointed. This means our dealings with every Christian we come across must be based on the consideration that they are children of God. We cannot afford to treat them shabbily. God is jealously guarding His own. As God's children, we have been bought with a price and the blood He has shed can never be in vain.

Often, we allow our past mistakes to hold us captive to a self-destructive lifestyle or keep us stuck, not going forward as God will have us. When we find ourselves in this not-so-great place, let us remember whose we are and understand that He is always willing to clean us up and give us the strength to move on. So, let our hearts be filled with the knowledge that we are children of the Most High God, and we can truly "chillax". Our God is not partial; He did this for our father, Abraham, the father of faith. When father Abraham feared for his life, he asked his wife Sarah to lie (to say that she was his sister), but our God had mercy on Abraham and intervened before King Abimelech touched Sarah. (Full account is in Genesis 20:1-16).

Our Good God is indeed mindful of us and will, in His Sovereignty, ensure everything works out for our good.

DAY THIRTEEN

Let us keep our focus on God

In Ephesians 3:20 (New Living Translation), we read:

Now all glory to God, who is able, through his mighty power at work within us, to accomplish infinitely more than we might ask or think.

There are a couple of Old Testament stories that help us see how keeping our focus on God will eventually lead to outstanding outcomes even if the journey is complex and full of unwanted bumps and troubles.

The first account is that of King David. The Book of First Samuel, chapter 30, tells how David and his men returned to their base camp in Ziklag (they had been turned away from helping the Philistine king fight Israel—this is a story for another day).

When David and his men got to Ziklag, they found their families and all their property taken away and their camp razed to the ground. David and his men were very distraught. There was even talk of stoning David (as the leader who had not made provisions to protect those left behind), but we are told that David *"encouraged himself in the LORD his God"* and asked God for direction. Then, on Jehovah's instructions and encouragement, David took some of his men to go and reclaim their families and property.

A tiny but essential part of this account is that David and his men stopped and helped a man they saw needed help on their way to reclaim what was taken. They could have left him there with the justifiable excuse that they were all hurting, and there was a sense of urgency (they had to find out where the invaders had taken their families and property). Hence, time was of the essence since the invading party may be on the move. We know that this man they stopped to help was instrumental in telling them where the invading army was, and David was able to go and completely retrieve all who were taken and their property as well.

The second account is about Joseph; we see this same mindset (Joseph's story is told in Genesis chapters 39 to 50). During his journey in life, Joseph found himself in prison through no fault of his own. He really was an innocent man, imprisoned for staying on the side of truth.

Joseph found two of his inmates sad and depressed, but rather than join the pity party, he chose to cheer them up. This involved decoding the dreams they had dreamt the previous night. The interpretation of the dreams happened just as Joseph had predicted. One of the inmates was released, and the other lost his life.

This act of choosing to cheer his inmates up and help them out of their sad situation rather than join in the pity party, ultimately led to Joseph being released from prison (it took a while, though—two years). Joseph was released from prison and became a very prestigious man, second only to the Pharaoh.

These men, David and Joseph, looked up to God even when things were not going well for them, and they were, therefore, able to look beyond their distress and comfort those around them who were hurting.

This type of mindset can only be attributed to God's power working on the heart and mind of man. We are naturally selfish; the prophet Jeremiah proclaims in Jeremiah 17:9:

'The heart is deceitful above all things and beyond cure. Who can understand it?'

Therefore, it takes drawing from God's power to have the ability to look beyond ourselves, regardless of what we are going through. It takes His strength to focus on what God has called us to do: reaching out to those who need us and require a touch of God's hand. Then, as we go about helping other people, we will surely tap into the solutions to our own problems.

David's story in 1 Samuel 30 is similar to the account of Jesus feeding over five thousand men, not counting women and children, as told in Matthew chapter 14. On learning about the killing of his cousin, John, Our Lord Jesus Christ made His way to a quiet place to reflect and grieve. But a crowd spotted Him and followed Him. Jesus would have been justified to ask them to give Him some time alone. Instead, He paused His need and ministered to the crowd, performing a miracle of multiplication in the process.

The Psalmist declares that *"the righteous person may have many troubles, but the LORD delivers him from them all"* (Psalm 34:19).

No matter what we go through, God will deliver us from them. David returned richer and more prosperous. Joseph became a great and wise ruler. Our challenges will not leave us where we are; we will not be stuck. Instead, as we look onto God and tap on His great comforting power, we will end up in a better, more fulfilling place than before we faced the challenge.

We must always turn to things that will bring us closer to God—this can be His Word, our place of prayer, songs of praise, and worship—whatever it is that will help us stay focused on God's power and not our present challenge.

And as sure as day follows night, we will have overwhelming testimonies of God's deliverance and provision.

DAY FOURTEEN

Our Gifts Make Way - 1

The story of Joseph told in Genesis 39 to 50 tells the account of a young man (Joseph) with a dream—a dream to lead and rule. However, on his way to fulfilling this dream, he encountered many mega obstacles—the betrayal of his brothers who sold him off as a slave, and the fury of his slave master's wife, whose sexual advances he rebuffed, which sent him to prison. While in prison, he comforted and supported his inmates, one of whom whose release he predicted (from interpreting a dream). Joseph asked this inmate, Pharaoh's wine bearer, to bring his plight of unjust imprisonment to Pharaoh when he got out, but he promptly forgot.

However, we see that Joseph was released at some point and went straight from being a prisoner to becoming the second in command to Pharaoh, having equal if not more control of the nation than Pharaoh.

What was Joseph's ticket to this greatness? How did this happen? A passage in Luke's account of the martyr, Stephen's speech in the Acts of Apostles says:

[9] *"These patriarchs were jealous of their brother Joseph, and they sold him to be a slave in Egypt. But God was with him* [10] *and rescued*

him from all his troubles. And God gave him favour before Pharaoh, king of Egypt. God also gave Joseph unusual wisdom, so that Pharaoh appointed him governor over all of Egypt and put him in charge of the palace (Acts 7:9-10).

The question of how Joseph went from being a prisoner to becoming the prime minister in about 24 hours is found in verse 10 in the passage above. *"...And **God gave him favour before Pharaoh, king of Egypt**. God **also gave Joseph unusual wisdom, <u>so</u>** that **Pharaoh appointed**..."*

We are all on different routes on our various journeys, but we are all taking the same bus, the bus called LIFE. It is not a free ride, and we need the ticket called 'God's Favour' to get off at the right, fruitful, and profitable destination.

Joseph's ride to his destination—Prime Minister of the Egyptian Empire at that time, had some major, life-shaking turbulence, but he made it. He was not only ruler over Egypt, but he was also ruler over Pharaoh's palace. He had control of Pharaoh's intimate affairs. This truly is double honour following a period of shame! Joseph's honour was restored such that the pain of his journey was ameliorated.

As we read Joseph's story, we can't but take note that at each junction of his life, we are told, *'but God was with him'*. As unlikely as it sounds, God was with him in the pit (where his brothers dumped him). God was with him in his slave master's house, in prison, and as a prime minister. No matter where he found himself, God was with him, and Joseph knew and acknowledged this, even if he did not understand why this journey was taking this route and whether he would get to his desired destination. Being aware that God was with him enabled Joseph to remain authentic to the person God called him to be. He remained a kind man of integrity, following and doing God's bidding.

Similarly, as long as we are aware that God is always on our side, we will be able to look at the turbulence we are passing through on our own journeys and take courage and comfort that our God, who is the same yesterday, today, and forever, will land us safely at our various destinations. We can afford to disregard whatever oppositions are rising against us and remain authentic to who God called us to be.

The One who made and controlled heaven and earth is with us. He will deliver us and give us wisdom and favour to triumph where our detractors had intended destruction. Just like Joseph, we will receive double honour at that very juncture. We will be completely vindicated.

DAY FIFTEEN

Our Gifts Make Way - 2

A gift opens the way and ushers the giver into the presence of the great (Prov. 18:16).

How did Joseph obtain this ticket (God's favour and wisdom) for his journey? A journey that saw him launch from prisoner to prime minister, in control of the country and the chambers of the most powerful king of that era. I believe the token that enabled Joseph to obtain his ticket is the gift God gave him. He had a gift, and he was willing to present the gift when it was needed.

Genesis 40 and 41 tell the story of two fellow inmates who had troubling dreams that depressed them. They had offended Pharaoh and were, therefore, sentenced to a term in jail. They deserved their sentences, but Joseph, on the other hand, had been wrongfully accused and was innocent of the charges levied against him. If anyone had the 'right' to depression and self-pity, it was Joseph. Yet, when he saw his fellow inmates were sad, he sought to cheer them up. He willingly offered his gift of dream interpretation to his inmates to encourage them. Not grudgingly but willingly.

It will appear that Joseph, despite his turbulent journey, had kept close fellowship with God and fixed his gaze on Jehovah. He had put his faith and hope on God's word to him and would endeavour to stay on the side of truth and integrity.

He said to his master's wife, who was relentlessly pursuing him for sex, *"... how then can I do such a wicked thing and sin against God?"* (Genesis 39:9). To his fellow inmates who were puzzled, confused, and depressed over the dreams they had dreamt, he said, *"...do not interpretations belong to God? Tell me your dreams..."* (Genesis 40:8). Joseph interpreted the dreams; the wine-bearer was freed, while the baker was executed for his crimes.

Joseph had asked the wine-bearer to tell Pharaoh about the injustice done to him; however, the wine-bearer promptly forgot in the joy and celebrations that heralded his release from prison.

We will not be far wrong to conclude that despite the vicissitudes of life Joseph faced, he kept his focus and gaze on God. It is so easy to imagine Joseph echoing the Psalmist and saying, *"I wait for the Lord, my whole being waits and, in His word, I put my hope"* (Psalm 130:5). We can imagine this being Joseph's mantra as he faced a turbulent uncertain journey.

It took another two years for his vindication and exaltation to come, but when it did, God made him forget all his troubles—hence, he named his first son, **Manasseh**, which sounds like the Hebrew word, *'forget'*.

It will be worth mentioning that when Joseph got this gift and entered the bus of his life's journey, it would have seemed it was the wrong bus he got into. It was the gift of dreams that got Joseph's brothers to act on their jealously and take the decision to sell him off as a slave. Joseph must have realised this gift was from God and was therefore not reluctant to use (present) this gift when it was needed. He did not hold a grudge against God and pack his gift away. Instead, he acquired the wisdom to guide himself in presenting it for the good of others and not for self-aggrandisement.

God has given every one of us a gift, and we need to identify it. It is through our gifts we obtain our tickets (God's favour and wisdom) to enter the right bus for our life's journey.

When it seemed, the circumstances had the upper hand in silencing Joseph, God orchestrated a situation that would re quire his gift. He is the same God yesterday, today, and forever. The Bible informs us that we are collectively the Body of Christ. He has given us different gifts which we are to use to bless others (Rom. 12:3-8). Our constant goal is to learn how to give these gifts out with a generous heart and spirit. In doing so, we will receive the tickets (favour and wisdom) to embark on the right bus for our life's journeys. This journey will ultimately end in the very presence of Jehovah God Himself, the great 'I AM that I AM'. There's plenty of room on the bus. When the bus stops right in front of our door, all we need to do is present our gift to the driver, our Lord Jesus Christ, and get our ticket (favour and wisdom) to enable us to embark on this life's journey.

Enlargement Against the Odds

We remain with Joseph's story and explore some questions afresh, "How did Joseph get from a place of slavery and criminal record (unjust, though it was) to a place of high significance, influence, and consequence?" "How did Joseph, who had been completely stripped of his identity and self-worth (he had been sold as a slave), end up as one whose word was law, who had people's livelihood in his hands, and one who was sought after at a great price?"

When Joseph was released from prison and went before Pharaoh, Pharaoh said to Joseph, *"You shall have charge over my house, and all my people shall be governed according to your word [with reverence, submission, and obedience]. Only in matters of the throne will I be greater than you are." Then Pharaoh said to Joseph, "See, I have set you over all the land of Egypt..."* (Genesis 41:40-41; AMP).

In summary, how did Joseph's sphere of influence enlarge beyond the imaginable in a twinkle of an eye? I believe the following scripture holds the answer for us.

"For we are God's [own] handiwork (His workmanship), recreated in Christ Jesus, [born anew] that we may do those good works which

God predestined (planned beforehand) for us [taking paths which He prepared ahead of time], that we should walk in them [living the good life which He prearranged and made ready for us to live]" (Ephesians 2:10; AMP).

The answer embedded in the passage above is not as far-fetched as we may think. There is some scriptural precedence to explore first. As a young man in his teens, Joseph had two similar dreams in content and inference. God spoke to him twice about the same thing. In biblical numerology, the number '2' means to witness and support. John records in John 8:17 that Jesus said the following, *"In your own law, it is written that the testimony of two witnesses is true."*

Pharaoh had two dreams, and Joseph confirmed to Pharaoh that these dreams were 'one and the same'. Therefore, God has revealed to Pharaoh what He is about to do (Genesis 41:25). Joseph had two dreams as a teenager, the interpretation of which depicted him as one who would rule and be in authority over his family, including his parents. Therefore, we can infer that God will orchestrate events to see Joseph's dreams come true, no matter what. God, who knows the end from the beginning, had a divine purpose for Joseph and nothing was going to stand in the way of Joseph achieving that purpose. Joseph's purpose was, *'...the saving of many lives...'* (Genesis 50:20).

So, God had a purpose, 'work prepared in advance' for Joseph to do. For this purpose, God was with Joseph and *'enabled him to gain the goodwill and favour of Pharaoh king of Egypt.'* It was a journey of over 13 years, but Joseph got to where he was meant to reach. In the same manner, I'm certain so shall we. We will get to that place of blessing and flourishing, and we will be a delight to ourselves.

The Sovereign and Providential God will orchestrate the circumstances around us to bring us to an expected end—the place of fulfilment. As children of the Most High God, who has received Christ Jesus as our Lord and Saviour, God has a purpose for us, one that will lead us to enlarge our sphere of influence despite any odds we may encounter in the course of fulfilling that purpose. As He was with Joseph, so is He with us. He will deliver us from all our *'distressing afflictions'* and bring us to our expected end and place of blessing. God will be with us, remembering us always, to bless our families and us.

To borrow some words from the Psalmist,

And let God bless all who fear God—bless the small, bless the great. Oh, let God enlarge your families—giving growth to you, growth to your children. May you be blessed by God, by God, who made heaven and earth (Psalm 115:13-15; The Message).

We will be blessed.

Thanks to our Lord Jesus Christ

The Gift that our Lord Jesus Christ is cannot be quantified or fully described. The Gift that He is and all that He pours into us are too wonderful for words. He gives a sure hope, one that '...*will not lead to disappointment...*' (Romans 5:5; NLT)

Our Lord Jesus Christ took the walk to the cross, to that horrible, blood-curdling crucifixion. The earth shook, the ground rocked, a tomb was carved out, a body was buried, and a heavy stone was used as a seal with soldiers on guard. It appears all hope was lost, and the expectation of a new Kingdom was dashed. The promise of a new life, new home, and new order rapidly faded, but...the word 'but' is very significant here. But Jesus Christ rose from the grave and once again established this 'certain hope' that will not disappoint us. The empty grave on that first Resurrection morning restored hope, confidence, and certain victory.

Jesus Himself let us know this sequence of events will happen. He told His disciples, "*I tell you the truth, you will weep and mourn over what is going to happen to me, but the world will rejoice. You will grieve, but your grief will suddenly turn to wonderful joy. It will be like a woman suffering the pains of labour.*

When her child is born, her anguish gives way to joy because she has brought a new baby into the world. So, you have sorrow now, but I will see you again; then you will rejoice, and no one can rob you of that joy…" (John 16:20-22; NLT)

Our Lord Jesus Christ said, *'No one can rob you of that joy'*. Indeed, no one can rob us of the joy of our certain hope. If we remember nothing, we must not forget this: no matter what, no one can rob us of our joy! So, no matter where we are on the spectrum of life's emotions, feelings, or circumstances, one thing is certain, 'The tomb is empty'! The resurrection of our Lord Jesus Christ confirms our 'certain hope'. This certain hope tells us, in plain language, that if we are …

…plagued with guilt from our past – The Cross means that God's righteous anger against sin and sinners has been satisfied; the price has been paid.

…frustrated with our inability to please God – The Cross means that Jesus has fulfilled all the righteousness of the law because He has perfectly pleased His Father; those of us who are in Christ are also pleasing to God.

…struggling to be free from sinful bondage and addictions – The Cross and the empty tomb mean we do not have to continue in sin; the power of sin is broken.

…in circumstances that seem hopeless – The resurrection means that there is hope amid every circumstance.

The Resurrection means that God is all-powerful, and nothing is beyond His control. So, let us lift our heads up and see the eternal hope, that powerful hope which will not disappoint, and as Apostle Paul prayed,

"I pray that your hearts will be flooded with light so that you can understand the confident hope He has given to those He called—His holy people who are His **rich and glorious inheritance.** I also pray that you will understand the **incredible greatness of God's power for us who believe Him.** This is the **same mighty power that raised Christ from the dead** and seated Him in the place of honour at God's right hand in the Heavenly realms. Now He is far above any ruler or authority or power or leader or anything else – not only in this world but also in the world to come. God has put all things under the authority of Christ and has made Him **head over all things for the benefit of the church.** And the church is his body; it is made full and complete by Christ, who fills all things everywhere with himself... (Ephesians 1:18-23; NLT) – *Emphasis, mine.*

Everything Works out Right in the End

Life happens—the good, the bad, and the ugly. The assurance we have as children of God is that the vicissitudes of life do not defeat us. Our great and mighty Jehovah gives us the wisdom, power, and ability to navigate to a place of victory, joy, and peace.

Someone once said, "Just as fire purifies silver in the smelting process, trials refine our character. They bring us new and deeper wisdom, helping us discern truth from falsehood and giving us the discipline to do what we know is right. Above all, these trials help us realise that life is a gift from God to be cherished, not a right to be taken for granted."

When we, the children of the Most-High God, find ourselves in a place of adversity, God's mercy and rescuing grace kick in. He works all things out for our good and leaves us in a better shape than the trouble that met us.

Apostle Peter captures this very succinctly when he says,

"And after you have suffered a little while, the God of all grace [Who imparts all blessing and favour], Who has called you to His

[own] eternal glory in Christ Jesus, will Himself complete and make you what you ought to be, establish and ground you securely, and strengthen, and settle you" (1 Peter 5:10; AMP).

God Himself will bring us to a place of rich fulfilment and abundance. We only need to keep the faith. Remember, He who called is faithful. He will equip, strengthen, and watch over us. Just as He did for Joseph, He granted him favour and wisdom to navigate the tough terrain he found himself. So, God is able and willing to do the same for us. Note also that Joseph kept the faith. He kept his dream in focus and refused to see himself as a slave or dwell in the self-pity of a wrongly convicted prisoner. Therefore, he was able to act as God would have him do. He refused the advances of Potiphar's wife. He was also able to bypass his pain and minister to others.

The Psalmist reminds us,

"You have caused men to ride over our heads; We went through fire and through water; But You brought us out to rich fulfilment" (Psalm 66:12; NKJV).

We have our Lord Jesus Christ to look up to. He looks out for us; therefore, we can confidently look to Him to get the grace and mercy required in our time of need, knowing that whatever brand of 'flood' or 'fire' we are going through, the all-seeing, all-powerful, all-knowing, and omnipresent God is on our side to bring us to a place of rich fulfilment and abundance.

Our Lord Jesus Christ will never allow us to stay in a dead-end situation. He will always **pull us out or through.**

Knowledge is Power

When life happens, especially in a world that is overtly and covertly opposed to God's moral compass, the tendency is to flow with the crowd for fear of being noticed as different and losing out on the bounty. However, the Prophet Daniel says to us,

"...but the people who know their God shall prove themselves strong and shall stand firm and do exploits for God" (Daniel 11:32; AMPC).

It is important that we are sure of our identity in Christ Jesus. This keeps us focused and free to face the priorities God has set for us. Our Lord Jesus is noted to have said,

"...Then you will know the truth and the truth will set you free" (John 8:32).

Knowing that we belong to Jesus Christ frees us to be who He called us to be and will ultimately empower us to do exploits for Him. By knowing the truth, we are free from all forms of oppression. By knowing God, we have eternal life and have God's love in us. We have Jesus in us.

So, when we say 'we know', what exactly do we know? How much do we know? How do we get about knowing?

Another Old Testament prophet said,

"...my people are destroyed by lack of knowledge. Because you have rejected knowledge, I also reject you as my priests; because you have ignored the law of your God, I also will ignore your children" (Hosea 4:6).

Prophet Hosea points out that not only are God's people liable to be destroyed for lack of knowledge, but we can also reject the knowledge being offered. This sounds very much like an oxymoron—how can we reject knowledge? How can we reject what we already know? We can reject knowledge by acting very contrary to what we know. This always leads to disaster and failure for the child of God. When this happens, we go into hyperdrive, trying to undo the wrong. We plead and pledge with God and people in authority.

The way not to fall into the trap of rejecting the knowledge God will have us acquire is to stay with His word and wait for Him to prove Himself. When this happens, we will have the confidence of Prophet Elisha. In 2 Kings 6, we read the story of the Aramean army who were blinded at Elisha's command and led to the King of Israel. The King of Israel asked to kill the invading army (now blind), but Elisha objected. Why? Elisha knew he had control over this army—there was no point killing them since he could make them do what he wanted.

The Apostle John tells the story of a man who was blind from birth; he had an encounter with our Lord Jesus Christ and was healed and could see (John 9). He knew whose intervention led to him receiving his sight. This knowledge emboldened him, and when the Jewish elders at the time threatened him, he was not fazed by their threats.

In Apostle Peter's words, *'We have everything we need for a godly life through our knowledge of Him'* (our Lord Jesus Christ). Therefore, it goes without saying that for us to walk in the power of knowledge Jesus Christ brings, we must invest in the time to know Him.

Tests become Testimonies

There is a story commonly told about two hunters, let's call them Ken and Charles. The story goes thus:

An organization in Montana offered a bounty of $50.00 to anyone who catches a wolf alive. Two hunters named Ken and Charles decided to head to the hills and make some money capturing wolves. Day and night, they scoured the mountains and forest searching for their valuable prey. Exhausted after three days of hunting without any success, they both fell asleep. During the night, Sam suddenly woke up to find that they were surrounded by a pack of 50 wolves with flaming red eyes and bared teeth, snarling at the two hunters and preparing to pounce. Ken tapped Charles and said: "Hey, wake up; we are going to be rich".

The lesson from this story is that when we are surrounded by what appears to be many difficulties, we may, in fact, be surrounded by many opportunities.

In Genesis 22:1-2, we read about a dire season in Father Abraham's life:

"¹ Sometime later God tested Abraham. He said to him, "Abraham!"

"Here I am," he replied.

² Then God said, "Take your son, your only son, whom you love — Isaac — and go to the region of Moriah. Sacrifice him there as a burnt offering on a mountain I will show you."

This was to test Abraham's faith; did he really know God? Did he believe what God had said to him about his son, Isaac, that is, He will make His agreement with Isaac continue forever?

So, how did Abraham view this test? Abraham knew God's voice; there had been several conversations between God and Abraham. So, Abraham knew it was God speaking. Abraham also trusted God enough to know somehow God would fulfil His word concerning Isaac, even if it meant raising Isaac from the dead. The writer of Hebrews confirms this by saying,

"¹⁷⁻¹⁸ God tested Abraham's faith. God told him to offer Isaac as a sacrifice. Abraham obeyed because he had faith. He already had the promises from God. And God had already said to him, "It is through Isaac that your descendants will come." But Abraham was ready to offer his only son. He did this because he had faith. ¹⁹ He believed that God could raise people from death. And really, when God stopped Abraham from killing Isaac, it was as if he got him back from death" (Hebrews 11:17-19; Easy-to-Read Version).

The tests and their accompanying testimonies we encounter prove to us that God truly exists. We not only go through tests, but we will also go through trials. Tests are situations orchestrated to see if we have what it takes to progress—as in an examination. On the other hand, trials are unexpected, trying situations we go through—for instance, being diagnosed with a life-limiting disease. Whether tests or trials, they come to prove God's power in our lives and make us more patient, better developed Christians who are fully satisfied in Christ. Indeed, knowledge and words are crucial to turning our tests and trials into testimonies. Father Abraham demonstrated this perfectly; he knew God's Word was inviolable, and he got the reward for being obedient and trusting—acting in faith.

I pray God gives us the same grace to stand on God's word in the face of our trials and tests. If we do, we will definitely have testimonies to the glory of God.

The lyrics of an old Christian classic song by Andraé Crouch say,

I've had many tears and sorrows, I've had questions for tomorrow, there's been times I didn't know right from wrong. But in every situation, God gave me blessed consolation, that my trials come to only make me strong.

I've been to lots of places, I've seen a lot of faces, there's been times I felt so all alone. But in my lonely hours, yes, those precious lonely hours, Jesus lets me know that I was His own.

Through it all, through it all, I've learned to trust in Jesus, I've learned to trust in God.

Through it all, through it all, I've learned to depend upon His Word.

Look up, then Move Forward

The story of the Israelites at the Red Sea is a great one. It shows God's mighty power and faithfulness. We find this story in the Book of Exodus 14.

A lot of events preceded and followed this great incident. First, it is important to note that God had told Abraham there would come a time when his descendants would be enslaved, but God will deliver them:

[13] *Then the Lord said to him, "Know for certain that for four hundred years your descendants will be strangers in a country not their own and that they will be enslaved and mistreated there.* [14] *But I will punish the nation they serve as slaves, and afterward they will come out with great possessions* (Genesis 15:13-14).

Fast forward to Exodus 14—a lot of display of God's power had already taken place. Now, at the point of being completely free, the Israelites find themselves between a sea and a ravaging, mighty Egyptian army, smarting from their loss.

The Israelites found themselves between the proverbial 'rock and a hard place'; which way to go? They panicked, the Egyptians rejoiced, and God acted!

[13] Moses answered the people, "Do not be afraid. Stand firm and you will see the deliverance the Lord will bring you today. The Egyptians you see today you will never see again. [14] The Lord will fight for you; you need only to be still."

[15] Then the Lord said to Moses, "Why are you crying out to me? Tell the Israelites to move on (Exodus 14:13-15).

When Moses raised the staff, the Red Sea parted, and the Israelites walked on dry ground towards the Promised Land.

This story is the same for us today. We may rejoice in a great victory and escape to find ourselves seemingly trapped at the next huddle. It is important to know that as blood-bought and washed children of God, we are not immune to life's challenges. Life happens, but in Christ, we are equipped for victory. We must put in our hearts and minds the following promise from God Himself, recorded by Prophet Isaiah:

"Do not be afraid, for I have ransomed you. I have called you by name; you are mine. When you go through deep waters, I will be with you. When you go through rivers of difficulty, you will not drown. When you walk through the fire of oppression, you will not be burned up; the flames will not consume you. **When you're between a rock and a hard place, it won't be a dead end.** For I am the LORD, your God, the Holy One of Israel, your Saviour..." (Isaiah 43:1-2; MSG – Emphasis, mine).

With this firmly ingrained in our hearts and minds, we must believe God who has called us will not let us remain in a 'dead-end' situation, and He says to us, "All that stands in your way, I will use to showcase My glory, I will use to prove to you and those watching that I have got your back. You are Mine; I paid a huge price for you, I am not about to let you go, you belong to Me!"

So, let us understand that no matter how long or fraught the path we are treading, our God, who kept a 430-year-old promise, is faithful and will keep His promises to us. All we have to do when we find ourselves between a rock and a hard place is keep calm and not be consumed with fear. We must keep our minds on His promises and not allow our eyes to roam in a hundred directions seeking unreliable solutions or think up a dozen incomplete solutions.

We simply need to stop agitating and fretting. All we need to do is be still in His presence and wait for Him. While waiting, we can spend the time reminding Him that we trust Him, and His Glory is at stake, and then we take a step forward.

Breaking Through – God's Way

When life happens, especially when we are being severely challenged, we seek a breakthrough in the situation. How can we obtain this breakthrough? We do this by keeping focused on God's Word and power. We obtain the breakthrough by making spiritual progress and sustaining it. There are principles we need to be mindful of that will help us on our path of spiritual progress. A few of them are discussed below.

We need to understand that we are a work in progress. We shouldn't beat ourselves black and blue when facing challenges that seem to floor us repeatedly. There are encouraging words from the Book of Proverbs:

"For the lovers of God may suffer adversity and stumble seven times but they will continue to rise over and over again..." (Proverbs 24:16; The Passion Translation).

David also encourages us in one of his psalms:

23 The Lord makes firm the steps of the one who delights in Him;
24 though he may stumble, he will not fall for the Lord upholds him with His hand (Psalms 37:23-24).

We must learn to pick ourselves up and keep on, knowing that our God will not let us stay down.

Understand that Christ has taken hold of you. There's an account in the Book of Exodus that describes how Jehovah God protected the Israelites as they left Egypt:

[19] Then the angel of God, who had been traveling in front of Israel's army, withdrew and went behind them. The pillar of cloud also moved from in front and stood behind them, [20] coming between the armies of Egypt and Israel. Throughout the night the cloud brought darkness to the one side and light to the other side; so neither went near the other all night long (Exodus 14:19-20).

Jesus tells us in the Book of John that whoever the Father gives Him, He will receive and not drive away (John 6:37). Therefore, it will not be far-fetched for us to infer that one of the reasons the angel of the Lord and cloud moved behind the Israelites was to ensure no Israelite took matters into their own hands and decamped. God has taken hold of us, and we need to stay connected to Him. To stay connected is to be obedient and do what Jesus has asked us to do. Jesus said we are His friends if we do what He commands (John 14:15). God will surely do all to keep us with Him, but in His authenticity, He made us in His image. This means we have a will of our own, a will to say, 'Yes' or 'No'. Our part is to keep hold of Christ as He takes hold of us, and we will progress spiritually and see breakthroughs in thorny situations.

Don't focus on the past - Paul had reason to forget the past—he had held the coats of those who had stoned Stephen—the first Christian martyr (Acts 7:57-58). We have all done things for which we are ashamed, and we live in the tension of what we have been and want to be. Because our hope is in

Christ, we can let go of past guilt and look forward to what God will help us become. We must receive grace, not to dwell on our past. Instead, we should grow in the knowledge of God by concentrating on our relationship with Him now. We have been forgiven, and we must always have that fact and truth in the forefront of our minds. Then, we should move on to a life of faith and obedience, looking forward to a fuller and more meaningful life because of our hope in Christ.

Live in and by the victories you have already attained. Wherever we are on life's spectrum of highs and lows, we need to keep living in obedience to the light God has shown us and seek Him for more. If God has dealt with some sins in our lives, we must not slip back into it again. If He has cleaned out a dirty closet of our life, let us not start throwing the junk back in.

As we walk our way through these principles, let the words of Apostle Paul to the Philippian church encourage us:

"12 Not that I have already obtained all this, or have already arrived at my goal, but I press on to take hold of that for which Christ Jesus took hold of me. 13 Brothers and sisters, I do not consider myself yet to have taken hold of it. But one thing I do: Forgetting what is behind and straining toward what is ahead, 14 I press on toward the goal to win the prize for which God has called me heavenward in Christ Jesus" (Philippians 3:12-14).

Jehovah's Indisputable Rewards

The story is told in the Book of Ruth about a young widow who left her culture and people and followed her widowed mother-in-law back to Bethlehem. Naomi, the mother-in-law, had migrated to Moab with her husband and two sons. Ruth, her daughter-in-law, stuck by her when she decided to return after losing her husband and sons. During their relationship, Ruth's attentiveness to her mother-in-law was observed, and a wealthy, prestigious farmer (who later became Ruth's husband) was so impressed that he said to Ruth:

12 May the Lord repay you for what you have done. May you be richly rewarded by the Lord, the God of Israel, under whose wings you have come to take refuge" (Ruth 2:12).

In response to Peter's question about what they will benefit, having left everything to follow Him, Jesus said,

"...29 And everyone who has left houses or brothers or sisters or father or mother or wife or children or fields for my sake will receive a hundred times as much and will inherit eternal life..." (Matthew 19:29).

The writer of Hebrews also lets us know that God rewards those who earnestly seek Him (Hebrew 11:6). It is amazing that we should be rewarded for being recipients of God's gracious mercy and lovingkindness. All we do should be in thanksgiving and a show of gratitude, but we see that our good and gracious God rewards us. How is this so, and what do we have to do to earn a reward?

The story retold below will throw some light on this:

"When I was a boy, my father, a baker, introduced me to the wonders of songs", tenor Luciano Pavarotti relates. "He urged me to work very hard to develop my voice. Arrigo Pola, a professional tenor in my hometown of Modena, Italy, took me as a pupil. I also enrolled in a teachers' college. On graduating, I asked my father, 'Shall I be a teacher or a singer?'

'Luciano,' my father replied, 'if you try to sit on two chairs, you will fall between them. For life, you must choose one chair.' "I chose one. It took seven years of study and frustration before I made my first professional appearance. It took another seven to reach the Metropolitan Opera. And now I think whether it's laying bricks, writing a book—whatever we choose—we should give ourselves to it."

Pavarotti's story (the advice his father gave him) practically demonstrates what Ruth and the Hebrew writer are telling us— commitment is the key to receiving a reward from God. Commitment to God is born out of obedience to Him.

To be committed to an endeavour requires a form of single-mindedness. We must learn to be single-minded in our pursuit of God and things concerning Him; then, the rewards will flow because our God is not unjust. He will not forget the love we have shown Him as we do what He has asked us to do. The rewards will come as we diligently, earnestly, and obediently seek to love our Father.

To be committed means we must focus on the key task God has asked or called us to (as in Pavarotti's case, 'choose one chair'). Focus is an important virtue. We will achieve nothing significant in life without it.

Ruth was single-minded about going to Bethlehem with her mother-in-law, Naomi. However, she was dedicated to serving the needs of Naomi and richly rewarded by marrying a man of distinction, Boaz, having a son who is mentioned as a direct ancestry of our Lord Jesus Christ.

In a world besieged with so many choices, means, and ways, we must learn to focus on the things God has called us to do. Be obedient to Him and eschew every distraction.

The Holy Spirit, who helps us all the time, especially in our moments of weakness, will enable us to stay focussed once we have made the requisite commitment. We can rely on Him to keep us on the path God has lined up for us, and we will then be able to receive and enjoy the rewards He so generously desires to give us.

This Life Called 'Farm'

Assume for a moment that 'life' is a huge field/farm. The thing about this farm (life) is that there are different types of soil formations, and the crops/plants are all at different stages of the harvesting continuum. That is to say; the soil is just being tilled in one section of the farm. Seeding is taking place at another section of the farm; yet another section is being weeded, and another is being harvested. This illustration refers to arable farming, but it can also apply to animal husbandry—the animals (poultry, piggery, dairy, etc.) are at different stages of development before being 'harvested' for food.

In order to remain 'well stocked', we need to ensure we have something to harvest. Therefore, our farm (life) should have sections which are always at the harvest stage, and for this to happen, there must be sections that are always at the planting state. If there is no planting, there cannot be a harvest.

In His unfathomable grace and favour, there are times when God allows us to harvest in sections we have not planted (someone else has done the planting). As a matter of fact, God told the Israelites, in the days of Joshua,

"...¹³ So I gave you a land on which you did not toil and cities you did not build; and you live in them and eat from vineyards and olive groves that you did not plant" (Joshua 24:13).

One thing we need to understand is that in the farm called life, if our harvest is to be successful, it must be at God's direction. Also, we can choose to use the seed He supplies or go to the section He has directed us to harvest. For instance, in the story of Ruth, she was providentially directed to a specific farm to glean (pick up left-over grain during the harvest). This farm happened to be Boaz's farm, who later married her, and Obed, King David's grandfather, was born.

When we heed God's direction, taking from the supply He gives us, then the following becomes true for us:

¹⁰ Now he who supplies seed to the sower and bread for food will also supply and increase your store of seed and will enlarge the harvest of your righteousness. ¹¹ You will be enriched in every way so that you can be generous on every occasion, and through us your generosity will result in thanksgiving to God (2 Corinthians 9:10-11).

There are times when we are called to do the sowing and reaping as well. However, whether we are gifted with a ripe field to harvest or have to nurture one ourselves, the end result if we use the supplies God gives us is one of success. If we choose other seeds rather than the one given to us by God, the consequences will be rather dire, as Apostle Paul informed the Galatian church:

⁷ Do not be deceived: God cannot be mocked. A man reaps what he sows. ⁸ Whoever sows to please their flesh, from the flesh will reap destruction; whoever sows to please the Spirit, from the Spirit will reap eternal life (Galatians 6:7-8).

It is crucial we see a clear distinction—the seed for planting is not the seed for food. We must understand this distinction so as not to eat our planting seeds.

Victory lies in us recognising the seed from the food, ensuring we sow the seed no matter what, to bring forth a harvest, rather than eat our seed and have nothing to sow and consequently miss out on a harvest.

When things get difficult and dire, how do we receive the strength and discipline to sow the planting seeds rather than eat them?

Our Master, Jesus Christ, shows us how. He resisted the temptation to throw away our seed of salvation when the devil tested Him. Matthew's account of this encounter reads as follows:

¹Then Jesus was led by the Spirit into the wilderness to be tempted by the devil. ² After fasting forty days and forty nights, he was hungry. ³ The tempter came to him and said, "If you are the Son of God, tell these stones to become bread."

⁴ Jesus answered, "It is written: 'Man shall not live on bread alone, but on every word that comes from the mouth of God.'"

⁵ Then the devil took him to the holy city and had him stand on the highest point of the temple. ⁶ "If you are the Son of God," he said, "throw yourself down. For it is written:

"'He will command His angels concerning You, and they will lift You up in their hands so that you will not strike your foot against a stone'"

⁷ Jesus answered him, "It is also written: 'Do not put the Lord your God to the test.'"

⁸ Again, the devil took him to a very high mountain and showed him all the kingdoms of the world and their splendour. ⁹ "All this I will give you," he said, "if you will bow down and worship me."

¹⁰ Jesus said to him, "Away from me, Satan! For it is written: 'Worship the Lord your God and serve him only.'"

¹¹ Then the devil left him, and angels came and attended him (Matthew 4:1-11).

At a tough time—starving after 40 days and nights of fasting, Jesus was able to hold His own against the devil. We cannot deny the fact that sowing can be a back-breaking exercise; it is then we should look up to God for strength. The values Jesus taught us by the way He handled the testing can be summed up as follows:

Our identity is in God – we must not lose it. The devil started by saying to Jesus, *if you are the Son of God*…Jesus knew who He was and was able to rebuff Satan. We are enabled to do the same by knowing that we are Christ's, and He has our best interest as His primary agenda.

Trust in God; let Him be our source for relief and elevation – God will always come through for His children. He did not spare His only Son, our Lord Jesus Christ, but gave Him up for us. He will, along with Jesus, gives us all things. So, our trust and source must be God alone. We must reject whatever we are offered outside God, no matter how glittering and pleasant it looks. At the end of the day, what God gives us cannot be compared to anything we get for ourselves. The angels and host of the angelic armies will guard the investment God has placed on us.

In a nutshell, we must sow our planting seeds, no matter what. Let us not use the seed to buy favour or position. Let us only look up to God as the source of our yield. There will always be enough harvest to see us through trying times.

The God-Ward Perspective

Duck or Rabbit – what do you see?

There's an ancient parable about a group of blind men who came across an elephant. None of them knew its shape or form, and they decided to inspect and know it by touch.

The first person whose hand landed on the trunk said, "This being is like a thick snake". For another one whose hand reached its ear, it seemed like a kind of fan. As for another person whose hand was upon its leg, the animal is a pillar like a tree trunk. The blind man who placed his hand upon its side said the elephant "is a wall". Another who felt its tail described it as a rope. The last felt its tusk, stating the elephant is that which is hard, smooth, and like a spear (adapted from Wikipedia).

Our perspective on life matters. There's an earlier story about two hunters who went hunting for wolves for payment for each wolf caught. They had spent three days and caught nothing; tired, they fell asleep. They were woken by wild-eyed, snarling wolves that had surrounded them. One of them wakes the other up and says, 'Wake up, we are rich'. Someone else would have seen certain death, but he saw prosperity.

As children of God, we also have to develop a God-ward perspective.

We read about a strong, determined, and God-fearing Israelite leader called Joshua. He had led Israel in many wars with outstanding victories. The Israelites were on their way to conquering the territories God had promised them. A group called the Gibeonites heard about the great victories Joshua and the Israelites had won and hatched a plot to avoid being annihilated. We read about this story in Joshua 9:

³ However, when the people of Gibeon heard what Joshua had done to Jericho and Ai, ⁴ they resorted to a ruse: They went as a delegation whose donkeys were loaded with worn-out sacks and old wineskins, cracked and mended. ⁵ They put worn and patched sandals on their feet and wore old clothes. All the bread of their food supply was dry and mouldy. ⁶ Then they went to Joshua in the camp at Gilgal and said to him and the Israelites, "We have come from a distant country; make a treaty with us."

⁷ The Israelites said to the Hivites, "But perhaps you live near us, so how can we make a treaty with you?"

⁸ "We are your servants," they said to Joshua.

But Joshua asked, "Who are you and where do you come from?"

¹² This bread of ours was warm when we packed it at home on the day we left to come to you. But now see how dry and mouldy it is. ¹³ And these wineskins that we filled were new, but see how cracked they are. And our clothes and sandals are worn out by the very long journey."

¹⁴ The Israelites sampled their provisions but did not inquire of the Lord.

In this story, Joshua looked at the facts presented to him but did not seek the truth from God. He was deceived into making a treaty with the Gibeonites, which meant Joshua could not attack them when he discovered he had been deceived. He had to honour the covenant he made with the Gibeonites. Sometime later, the Gibeonites were threatened by a coalition of armies. Because of the treaty, Joshua and Israel had to fight for them, and God gave them victory. Joshua got himself and the Israelites into a pickle; he looked at the facts but did not ascertain the truth. As children of God, whatever situation we find ourselves in, we can look at the facts of our circumstances but seek to find and acknowledge the truth. The truth can only be found in God's word.

Our Lord Jesus is the perfect example; the writer of Hebrews says,

¹ "… let us throw off everything that hinders and the sin that so easily entangles. And let us run with perseverance the race marked out for us, ² fixing our eyes on Jesus, the pioneer and perfecter of faith.

For the joy set before him he endured the cross, scorning its shame, and sat down at the right hand of the throne of God. ³Consider him who endured such opposition from sinners, so that you will not grow weary and lose heart." (Hebrews 12:1-3).

Our Lord Jesus Christ focussed on the truth of our salvation. He saw and understood the fact of the cross, but He scorned the shame and looked to the truth of our salvation and the joy our salvation will bring Him, and ultimately us.

Jesus Christ had a God-ward perspective, which brought about the salvation we enjoy today. Some people will sometimes make us believe that when we pass through difficulties, it is because we did not have the right attitude or we are in sin. If Jesus was distressed, troubled, and endured shame, what makes you think we will not pass through some kind of distress as well? Because we have Jesus, we can sail through whatever life throws our way. Jesus Christ could have decided that it was too much at the time and cut the suffering short, but He knew what it meant for Him to go to the cross. Jesus Christ endured the cross and its shame to fulfil the assignment He came to accomplish.

When we are faced with uncertainty, and it appears the outcome will be bleak, it may be fact, but the truth says God has a good plan for us—plans that will prosper us and give us hope and a future (Jeremiah 29:11). When we are troubled, we need to remember the words of our Lord Jesus Christ. He acknowledged we would have trouble in the world but declared the truth, that in Him, we would have His peace, not the peace the world gives, but His peace which passes all understanding (John 16:33; Philippians 4:7).

When we are facing trials of many kinds, that's a fact. But the truth is these trials are perfecting us, producing perseverance, and making us more mature, and in this, we can rejoice (James 1:2).

No matter what path or how long our journey in life takes us, as long as we walk and work with God, we will get to what He has purposed for us. When we see things from a God-ward perspective, our joy, peace, and sense of purpose remain intact because we are in Christ Jesus. We are assured that we are running a race we are destined to win.

Keep Winning

When we win a game or a war, we consider ourselves triumphant over that situation. We have overcome some sort of challenge, resistance, battle, conflict, or resolved some tension. We have moved or bypassed an obstacle.

The Bible is replete with King David's victories whenever he went to war. We know of the famous 'David versus Goliath' story. In most, if not all of his battles, David always asked God for direction. Whenever he faced a battle/war, he would ask God for direction. David did not base his confidence on his past victories or rely on the laurels of his previous wars. He would always ask God for direction and strategy. David's complete reliance and dependence on God's direction and leading are seen very clearly in the following portion of scripture:

¹ When David was told, "Look, the Philistines are fighting against Keilah and are looting the threshing floors," ² he inquired of the Lord, saying, "Shall I go and attack these Philistines?"

The Lord answered him, "Go, attack the Philistines and save Keilah."

³ But David's men said to him, "Here in Judah we are afraid. How much more, then, if we go to Keilah against the Philistine forces!"

⁴ Once again David inquired of the Lord, and the Lord answered him, "Go down to Keilah, for I am going to give the Philistines into your hand." ⁵ So David and his men went to Keilah, fought the Philistines and carried off their livestock. He inflicted heavy losses on the Philistines and saved the people of Keilah. ⁶ (Now Abiathar son of Ahimelek had brought the ephod down with him when he fled to David at Keilah.)

⁷ Saul was told that David had gone to Keilah, and he said, "God has delivered him into my hands, for David has imprisoned himself by entering a town with gates and bars." ⁸ And Saul called up all his forces for battle, to go down to Keilah to besiege David and his men.

⁹ When David learned that Saul was plotting against him, he said to Abiathar the priest, "Bring the ephod." ¹⁰ David said, "Lord, God of Israel, your servant has heard definitely that Saul plans to come to Keilah and destroy the town on account of me. ¹¹ Will the citizens of Keilah surrender me to him? Will Saul come down, as your servant has heard? Lord, God of Israel, tell your servant."

And the Lord said, "He will."

¹² Again David asked, "Will the citizens of Keilah surrender me and my men to Saul?"

And the Lord said, "They will."

¹³ So David and his men, about six hundred in number, left Keilah and kept moving from place to place. When Saul was told that David had escaped from Keilah, he did not go there (1 Samuel 23:1-13).

A long read, but it shows how clearly David did not rely on his men, strength, or the loyalty of the people of Keilah, whom he had delivered from the Philistine army. His dependence was on God.

In the Book of 2 Chronicles, chapter 20, we meet one of David's descendants, Jehoshaphat, the 6th king of the Kingdom of Judah. By the time Jehoshaphat came on the throne, the Kingdom of Israel had split into two. Israel to the north and Judah to the south.

Jehoshaphat received news that a coalition of five armies was making its way to attack him. Despite his fear and alarm at this great army coming against him, Jehoshaphat set aside time to seek God's face, and he called the whole nation of Judah to join him:

³ Alarmed, Jehoshaphat resolved to inquire of the Lord, and he proclaimed a fast for all Judah. ⁴ The people of Judah came together to seek help from the Lord; indeed, they came from every town in Judah to seek him (2 Chronicle 20:3-4).

Jehoshaphat's prayer and subsequent actions are recorded in verses 5 to 29 of 2 Chronicles 20.

The good news is that God gave Jehoshaphat a strategy which led to victory. Jehoshaphat went to war with praise singers (sing praise to God) in the forefront. We are told that,

"²² As they began to sing and praise, the Lord set ambushes against the men of Ammon and Moab and Mount Seir who were invading Judah, and they were defeated."

God has a myriad of strategies up His sleeve, so it's always the best and wisest thing to seek His counsel when we face challenges and distressing situations. Sometimes, as in David's case, there was an actual battle. At other times as in Jehoshaphat's case, God Himself set the ambush, and the coalition turned on themselves and fought themselves. Jehoshaphat's army did not need to fight. Whatever strategy God chooses to give us, there are a few things we can adopt from Jehoshaphat's story to help us stay on the winning side.

King Jehoshaphat recognised the dire situation he was in; though alarmed and fearful of the facts facing him, he sought the truth from Jehovah God.

He recognised the limitations of his wisdom. None of us, regardless of our wisdom, can outsmart Satan.

He recognised his strength was insufficient against this coalition but knew and relied on the truth that God will keep His promise to His people. He had testimonies of what God had done in the past and had faith He will and could deliver them.

He recognised the all-sufficiency power of his God. He was wise because he locked his eyes on the One who had the power to deliver and save him.

Like Jehoshaphat, let us understand and keep our focus on God and seek His direction and guidance. Then, follow through on the strategies He gives us. The Sovereign God has a myriad of patterns and strategies at His disposal. He is the Way-maker; He brings forth springs of clean water in dry and arid places. He is God, and nothing is impossible for Him to do.

We can truly have perfect peace in the face of challenges because we serve a great and mighty God who assures us of victory.

We are running a race we are destined to win.

DAY TWENTY-SEVEN

Jehovah's Measuring Scale

The process the Prophet Samuel took to identify David, Jesse's son, as the next king of Israel after Saul is told in 1 Samuel 16. Saul, the first king of Israel, had messed up. He had demonstrated that he had more allegiance to what people said and thought about him than what God wanted him to do. As a result, God had identified a *'man after His own heart and appointed him leader'* (I Samuel 13:14) even before Prophet Samuel visited Jesse's family.

When Samuel arrived at Jesse's compound, he asked for all Jesse's sons to be presented so that God would choose the one who would be king. From the very beginning, God made it clear that His measuring yardstick was not the same as either Jesse's or Samuel's:

⁶When they arrived, Samuel saw Eliab and thought, "Surely the Lord's anointed stands here before the Lord."

*⁷But the Lord said to Samuel, "Do not consider his appearance or his height, for I have rejected him. **The Lord does not look at the things people look at. People look at the outward appearance, but the Lord looks at the heart"** (1 Samuel 16:6-7 – Emphasis, mine).*

Jesse presented seven of his sons, but God chose none of them. God had told Samuel earlier that He had chosen one of Jesse's sons to be king, so Samuel then asked Jesse if these were all his sons. It was only at this time Jesse remembered his last son, David. We can all speculate why David wasn't invited to the meeting from the start; could it be his age (too young) or his job (tending sheep)? Whatever, he clearly wasn't considered an option to be chosen by his father. But our God, who sees men's hearts and knows the end of a matter before the beginning, had made His choice. When Prophet Samuel realised there was still one more son, he asked Jesse to go get him and said, *"…we will not sit down until he arrives"* (1 Samuel 16:11).

We later find out David was God's choice, not a perfect human being by any standards, but one who was faithful to God and had a heart sold out to God; therefore, God's choice.

Our Lord Jesus Christ made a very interesting observation when He watched people giving their offerings into the temple treasury:

*41-44 Sitting across from the offering box, he was observing how the crowd tossed money in for the collection. Many of the rich were making large contributions. One poor widow came up and put in two small coins—a measly two cents. Jesus called his disciples over and said, "**The truth is that this poor widow gave more to the collection than all the others put together.** All the others gave what they'll never miss; she gave extravagantly what she couldn't afford—she gave her all"* (Mark 12:41-44 – Emphasis, mine).

It is very clear for us to see that God's measuring yardstick is not the same as ours. How can two measly cents be worth more than the thousands of dollars dropped by the rich?

Jesus says it's because she gave her all. She probably gave 90-95% of all she owned, and the others gave less than 1% of what they owned. Indeed, God does not define generosity in terms of quantity but measures of sacrifice.

Our Lord Jesus Christ corrected our misconception, judging the value of the gift by the quantity. The value of the widow's few pennies was worth more than a million pounds given by the rich who dropped their offering.

God expects us to give according to the measure we have been blessed by Him. Therefore, our generosity should be relative to our measure of blessing. God has blessed us in various ways—the gift of prophecy, service, teaching, encouraging, giving, leading, caring, and the list goes on. God expects that in dispensing these gifts (blessings), we'll do this diligently and cheerfully to the measure (degree) we have been blessed. We are channels of blessing, and the more we bless others with the gift God gave us, the more we are blessed, just as a running tap is kept wet when in use.

The quantity we present to God is irrelevant. A line from Danniebelle Hall's Song, "Ordinary People", says, "...little becomes much as you place it in the Master's hand."

When Jesus Christ was faced with more than 5000 hungry people, He was able to feed them to satisfaction with a young lad's meal of two fish and five loaves of bread, with more than twelve baskets of leftovers collected. God can multiply what we give Him. Jehovah's value of a gift is not based on the quantity you have given but on the proportion of the gift to the blessing you have.

We should also learn not to judge by the world's standards and judge people based on what they give. We should also not judge ourselves that way and hold back from giving because we think what we have will not measure up to what others give, whether it be time, money, or any other resource.

It is our choice to give what we are determined to give:

7 Each of you should give what you have decided in your heart to give, not reluctantly or under compulsion, for God loves a cheerful giver (2 Corinthians 9:7).

The Passion Translation interprets the above verse as follows,

"Let giving flow from your heart, not from a sense of religious duty. Let it spring up freely from the joy of giving—all because God loves hilarious generosity".

If we do not make an offering of our time, talents, and money to God, something else will take them away, denying us true satisfaction and godly rewards. We must remember that God will not leave us short-changed. He who supplies seed to the sower and bread for food will always provide our needs, no matter where we are. He will never let us down.

Let us learn to be cheerful, generous givers of our time, talent, and money. Whatever we have, let us give generously. God will ensure that we who are channels of these blessings will never run dry. His definition of generosity is not based on the quantity you give—so don't hold back.

DAY TWENTY-EIGHT

A Fresh Start

There are times in life when we wish we could start again, go back in time, make different decisions, be given a second chance, and have another go and undo some wrong. It's sometimes hard not to pitch our tents on the 'regret lane'. There's good news for those who are seeking a new beginning and would like to move on.

There's a very comforting portion of scripture:

17 Therefore, if anyone is in Christ, the new creation has come: The old has gone, the new is here! (2 Corinthians 5:17).

How awesomely brilliant it will be to live a life free of regret! This can only be possible with a life lived in Christ. The old is gone, and the new is here; the Message Bible says, *"...and what we see is that **anyone united with the Messiah gets a fresh start**, is created new. The old life is gone; a new life emerges!"* (*Emphasis, mine*).

The interesting fact is that even before Christ, God had demonstrated His generosity and kindness in giving His subjects a fresh start. In 2 Kings 20, we read about King Hezekiah, who had become ill and was at the point of death.

King Hezekiah gets a message from God through the Prophet Isaiah, asking him to put his house in order because he will not recover, but die from the sickness. On hearing this, King Hezekiah prayed earnestly to God and asked Him to reconsider, and He did. The Bible tells us that God added another 15 years to Hezekiah's life.

Another person of note we can consider is Apostle Peter. Peter was one of Jesus's closest disciples. Jesus took two others with him to the mount of transfiguration. He was with Jesus in the Garden of Gethsemane when Jesus was agonising and praying concerning His upcoming suffering and death. A shortcut of Peter's walk with Jesus enlightens us to the following.

Peter was a fisherman when Jesus met him and quickly rose through the ranks amongst the disciples of Jesus. Peter was present when Jesus preached and did many great miracles. Peter was used by the Holy Spirit to reveal who Jesus actually was. Things went reasonably well for Peter until Jesus was arrested. When the disciples deserted Jesus, Peter was at the forefront, swearing and cursing, denying that he ever knew our Lord Jesus Christ.

Following Jesus' resurrection, Peter and his friends were in a limbo of some sort. They knew Jesus had been raised from the dead; they had seen Him and shared some meals with Him. At one of these meals, our Lord Jesus Christ addresses Peter specifically. One evening, Peter and a few of the disciples, including Apostle John, Thomas, and Nathaniel, were together when Peter announced that he was going out to fish, and they all went with him. The Bible says, '...that night they caught nothing' (John 21:3).

Jesus appeared early in the morning and changed this scenario. He told them where to fish, and they caught such a great haul that they could not carry it into the boat. When they recognised it was Jesus who stood on the shore, Peter jumped into the water and swam ashore to Him.

When he and his friends reached the shore, they found that Jesus was already preparing them breakfast (fish, of course). When they had finished eating, Jesus then spoke to Peter,

¹⁵ *When they had finished eating, Jesus said to Simon Peter, "Simon son of John, do you love me more than these?"*

"Yes, Lord," he said, "you know that I love you."

Jesus said, "Feed my lambs."

¹⁶ *Again Jesus said, "Simon son of John, do you love me?"*

He answered, "Yes, Lord, you know that I love you."

Jesus said, "Take care of my sheep."

¹⁷ *The third time he said to him, "Simon son of John, do you love me?"*

Peter was hurt because Jesus asked him the third time, "Do you love me?" He said, "Lord, you know all things; you know that I love you."

Jesus said, "Feed my sheep. ¹⁸ *Very truly I tell you, when you were younger you dressed yourself and went where you wanted; but when you are old you will stretch out your hands, and someone else will dress you and lead you where you do not want to go."* ¹⁹ *Jesus said this to indicate the kind of death by which Peter would glorify God. Then he said to him, "Follow me!"* (John 21:15-19).

Our Lord Jesus Christ had predicted Peter's denial of Jesus. Jesus had told Peter that before the cock crows twice, Peter would deny Him three times. See how merciful our Lord Jesus Christ is? He reinstates Peter and reinforces Peter's purpose three times! For each time Peter denied Jesus, Jesus reinstated him. Jesus then turned to Peter and said, 'Follow Me' – giving Peter a fresh start.

This same Peter, who had denied Jesus, was the one who gave the first sermon in the Book of Acts, boldly declaring who Jesus is and inviting people to put their trust in Jesus and follow Him.

We can all experience a fresh start in our lives. Don't be conquered by the fear of failure; the resurrected Christ lives and gives us a fresh start to achieve beyond our expectations. Let us not be intimidated by frequent false starts. Let's look to the resurrected Christ and His Spirit. Even if history seems to be repeating itself, He stands and calls out to us, 'Friend', and says, 'try it my way—cast your net to the right!'

Now may God, the fountain of hope, fill us to overflowing with uncontainable joy and perfect peace as we trust in Him. And may the power of the Holy Spirit continually surround our lives with His super-abundance until we radiate with hope (Romans 15:13 – The Passion Translation).

We must not be cowered by the status quo and give up on our dreams. With the resurrected Christ, there is no dead situation. Instead, He stands at the shore, ready with a meal for strength and time of fellowship. He was freed from the agony of death; the grave could not hold Him down—so our hope will live forever, and we are always guaranteed a fresh start.

God Comforts Us

When life happens and leads us down a painful path, it is not uncommon for us to ask how or why our good and caring God allowed this to happen. Then, when the initial shock has abated, it is not unusual to begin to seek God's face in prayer for understanding, direction, and comfort.

Our Lord Jesus Christ, when He learnt that His cousin John had been murdered, He withdrew to be alone,

"¹² Later, John's disciples came for his body and buried it. Then they went and told Jesus what had happened.

¹³ As soon as Jesus heard the news, he left in a boat to a remote area to be alone..." (Matthew 14:12-13; New Living Translation).

When we get alone to speak to God, it is comforting to know we are before the Blessed Trinity. We come to the Father through the Son and in the power of the Holy Spirit—Apostle Paul, explaining this to the Ephesian church, said,

¹⁸ Now all of us can come to the Father through the same Holy Spirit because of what Christ has done for us (Ephesians 2:18; New Living Translation).

When we come to God, broken and seeking answers or solace, we are communicating with God, and the fact that we have access to the Triune God is humbling and enables us to prepare our hearts and hear what He will say to us.

These baffling and painful experiences, such as the sad loss of a child, a spouse who dies suddenly at the prime of their life, being ravaged by a disease that leads to the death of a loved one, an accident, or the loss of a job and income—the list is endless and can leave us really confused. It is assuring to know that we have access and can go to God in prayer for comfort, assurance, and direction. It is good to know that if we do, He hears us and will comfort us.

It is incredibly comforting to know that our God is patient with us and will wait until we get to Him. Some of us will seek comfort in all kinds of places, the latest TV sitcom, food, or the Internet. For some of us, it may be some caring friends who listen and try to understand our situation, but we can only lean on them so much, for we know they have their own lives and responsibilities. When we have exhausted our resources outside God and eventually turn to Him, we receive the blessed comfort the Prophet Isaiah promised:

"...For the Lord comforts his people and will have compassion on his afflicted ones" (Isaiah 49:13).

And Apostle Paul confirms this,

³ Praise be to the God and Father of our Lord Jesus Christ, the Father of compassion and the God of all comfort, ⁴ who comforts us in all our troubles, so that we can comfort those in any trouble with the comfort we ourselves receive from God (2 Corinthians 1:3-4).

That promise is for us all when we go through any kind of trouble. The Lord will give us the comfort we need. We must always turn to Him and pour out our hurt in prayer. He is always there for us.

We can say to Him, "I need your comfort today, Lord. The hurt goes deep. I need to know there is a purpose for this pain; I need to know that it will not be wasted. I need to feel the comfort that only you can give".

And He will always say to us, times without number, "I am there for you in your time of need. I will comfort you and have compassion on you".

The reliable, faithful, powerfully able and willing God will definitely bring us to our safe-landing place.

DAY THIRTY

Restoration and Healing in Our Lord Jesus Christ

The gospels are replete with accounts of healing and restorative miracles our Lord Jesus Christ performed when He was on earth. Luke records in the Book of Acts many healing miracles performed by the Apostles, and we have heard testimonies of people in our communities that our great and good God has healed or restored. God is still very much in the business of restoration and healing us today as He did in the past and recorded in the Old and New Testaments of the Bible.

Apostle Peter in 1 Peter 1:24 references one of the many prophecies about our Lord Jesus Christ when he says:

"²⁴ He personally carried our sins in his body on the cross so that we can be dead to sin and live for what is right. By his wounds you are healed" (New Living Translation).

Apostle James tells us to,

¹⁶ Confess to one another therefore your faults (your slips, your false steps, your offenses, your sins) and pray [also] for one another, that you may be healed and restored [to a spiritual tone of mind and heart]. The earnest (heartfelt, continued) prayer of a righteous man makes tremendous power available [dynamic in its working].

God's tremendous power is available to us today to bring about healing. He continues to and will perform miracles, miracles of healing and restoration in our lives. As we can see from what James says, we are partners with God in creating our miracles and reconciling the world back to God. That was why He gave us His Spirit, His nature, and His mind.

Restoration also includes the business of bringing back to life any dreams, hopes, aspirations, and whatever else we may have considered dead and buried. God expects us to play a part—after all, when He raised Lazarus from the dead, He left it to the people to roll away the stone and untie the grave clothes!

The Prophet Ezekiel tells of a great restoration for the Israelites:

¹The hand of the Lord was on me, and he brought me out by the Spirit of the Lord and set me in the middle of a valley; it was full of bones. ² He led me back and forth among them, and I saw a great many bones on the floor of the valley, bones that were very dry. ³ He asked me, "Son of man, can these bones live?"

I said, "Sovereign Lord, you alone know."

⁴ Then he said to me, "Prophesy to these bones and say to them, 'Dry bones, hear the word of the Lord! ⁵ This is what the Sovereign Lord says to these bones: I will make breath enter you, and you will come to life. ⁶ I will attach tendons to you and make flesh come upon you and cover you with skin; I will put breath in you, and you will come to life. Then you will know that I am the Lord.'"

⁷ So I prophesied as I was commanded. And as I was prophesying, there was a noise, a rattling sound, and the bones came together, bone to bone. ⁸ I looked, and tendons and flesh appeared on them and skin covered them, but there was no breath in them.

⁹ Then he said to me, "Prophesy to the breath; prophesy, son of man, and say to it, 'This is what the Sovereign Lord says: Come, breath, from the four winds and breathe into these slain, that they may live.'" ¹⁰ So I prophesied as he commanded me, and breath entered them; they came to life and stood up on their feet—a vast army.

¹¹ Then he said to me: "Son of man, these bones are the people of Israel. They say, 'Our bones are dried up and our hope is gone; we are cut off.' ¹² Therefore prophesy and say to them: 'This is what the Sovereign Lord says: My people, I am going to open your graves and bring you up from them; I will bring you back to the land of Israel. ¹³ Then you, my people, will know that I am the Lord, when I open your graves and bring you up from them. ¹⁴ I will put my Spirit in you and you will live, and I will settle you in your own land. Then you will know that I the Lord have spoken, and I have done it, declares the Lord'" (Ezekiel 37:1-14).

This prophecy gives us a clue into how we partner with God in bringing about healing and restoration into our ailing situations (including our health). We must do as Ezekiel did and speak God's truth to the facts. To follow Ezekiel's example,

We must speak the Word. When we speak God's Word into our situation, believing that what we have said will happen, God will make it happen for us. The gospel of Mark records Jesus Christ saying to us:

²³ "Truly I tell you, if anyone says to this mountain, 'Go, throw yourself into the sea,' and does not doubt in their heart but believes that what they say will happen, it will be done for them. ²⁴ Therefore I tell you, whatever you ask for in prayer, believe that you have received it, and it will be yours.

Let us learn to speak God's Word into our situations.

We must be specific. Ezekiel was instructed to speak to the bones and tell them specifically what will happen; breath will enter them, tendons will become attached, flesh will come upon them, and skin will cover them. We must speak to the structures that make up our situations and all the agencies standing in the way of us seeing the manifestation of God's promise to us.

We must be prepared to be persistent. Jesus told His disciples the story of a persistent widow who insisted on getting justice from an uncaring judge. She kept on at him until he heard her case. Jesus told them that the judge eventually yielded, saying, *"...yet because this widow keeps bothering me, I will see that she gets justice..."* (Luke 18:5). Until we see the complete manifestation of God's purposes for us, we must keep speaking God's Word to the situation. Our God is good and kind, and He desires to see us prosper and not come to harm. He has plans to give us hope and a future. He will give us the things we ask of Him.

God remains sovereign, and there are puzzling cases where the anticipated healing has not occurred. Still, we must continue to play our part and allow God to determine the outcome in His infinite wisdom and knowledge.

One thing is certain, our God has the power to make the impossible possible, and this power is at our disposal. Our God shows up on our behalf to bless and will continue to bless us. He will build us up and uplift us. He will not abandon us to the grave. Our Lord Jesus died and conquered the stranglehold of death by His resurrection, and this resurrection power assures us that there is no dead situation for the child of God.